Starting Secondary School

Michael Carr-Gregg is an adolescent psychologist, a well-respected speaker and one of Australia's leading authorities on teenage behaviour. In 1985 he founded CanTeen, the acclaimed cancer patients' support group for teenagers in New Zealand and Australia. He is the consultant psychologist to many schools and national organisations, and has written several books on parenting adolescents.

Sharon Witt has been immersed in teen world for almost three decades in her role as a secondary teacher, author and presenter to adolescents and their parents around the country. Sharon is the author of many books written for young people and is also the founder of the nationwide Resilient Kids Conference, a one-day conference aimed at equipping parents, educators and carers in building resilience in their children and teenagers.

Starting Secondary School

The essential handbook for every Australian family

Michael Carr-Gregg and Sharon Witt

UK | USA | Canada | Ireland | Australia
India | New Zealand | South Africa | China

Penguin Life is part of the Penguin Random House group of companies
whose addresses can be found at global.penguinrandomhouse.com.

Penguin
Random House
Australia

First published by Penguin Life, 2020

Online Family Safety Agreements (pp. 119–124) and Safety Tips for Parents (pp. 133–134)
used with permission CyberSafety Solutions, www.cybersafetysolutions.com.au

Cover photography by Gillian Vann/Stocksy
Cover design by James Rendall © Penguin Random House Australia Pty Ltd
Cartoons © Ivan Smith 2020
Typeset in 11/18 pt Sabon by Midland Typesetters, Australia
Colour separation by Splitting Image Colour Studio, Clayton, Victoria

Printed and bound in Australia by Griffin Press, part of Ovato, an accredited
ISO AS/NZS 14001 Environmental Management Systems printer

 A catalogue record for this
book is available from the
NATIONAL
LIBRARY   National Library of Australia
OF AUSTRALIA

ISBN 978 1 76089 408 5

We'd like to dedicate this book to all the fabulous young people who have graced our professional lives over the years and especially our own children, of whom we are immensely proud.

Contents

Introduction

Michael Carr-Gregg

Starting secondary school can be one of the most challenging transitions in a child's life. Leaving the familiar structure of primary school, with routines, guidelines and expectations that have been established over the previous seven years, is not to be underestimated.

Why can this transition feel so overwhelming? Let me paint you a picture.

Imagine you have just been given a brand-new job in a large office building. It is all completely foreign to you. You will be starting with anywhere from fifty to one thousand new employees, and you will have direct contact with perhaps fifty of those on a day-to-day basis. In addition, you will be expected to report to a range of supervisors at least once, sometimes several times, during the week, each having their own office in this large building.

On beginning your new role, you are given a timetable with set times pre-arranged for all meetings. In addition to this, each supervisor you report to will have their own unique personality and style that you will need to adjust to. They will most likely set tasks for you to complete at the end of each meeting and expect you to return these in a timely manner, probably at the next scheduled meeting.

Finally, you are expected to manage copious folders, books, stationery and equipment – many only required at specific meetings. You will need to take care of all your books, ensuring that those required for work completed at home are back with you the following day.

Oh, I might also add: lately you've been experiencing some huge changes going on in your body. Your feet have been growing at an alarming rate, you have hair growing in unfamiliar places, you often feel emotional for no apparent reason, and sleeping has been a problem for months.

This is what it is like for your child entering the unfamiliar territory of secondary school. Aside from getting to know an entirely new school environment, meeting a range of new teachers and students, and dealing with friendship issues, they are also expected to develop sound organisational skills, all while managing the usual stress and angst of being an early adolescent.

The reality is that this is a massive change in a child's life, when they leap from the safety of primary school into the deep murky waters of adolescence. It's a time when once-clear boundaries become blurred: parents are forced to take a step back, peers become far more influential, and family dynamics are completely blown apart. For many families, it's a time of having to deal with new conflict, being pushed right out of comfort zones, and living with someone you might find you don't even like very much anymore.

And in my experience, I know that many young people are struggling with the rigours and stresses of secondary school. In the most recent youth survey conducted by Mission Australia, in 2018, coping with stress and school or study problems consistently appear in the top three concerns of young people.

In 2014 there were almost 4.9 million young people aged 10–25 years in Australia. That's around one fifth of the population moving through puberty, adolescence and young adulthood. Though this period of growth has long been regarded as a challenging time for both teenagers and parents, 21st-century life has added some new ingredients into the mix.

You will note that I decided to write this book with a friend. Not just any friend but a superhero in the field of teaching, parent education, TV, radio and social media. Her name is Sharon Witt. I'm not sure she has a cape, but I have seen her teach and she definitely has pedagogical superpowers. I have been a big fan of hers for a long time. She brings to this book a robust practicality, sense of humour and wealth of school experience that I think parents will appreciate.

We've each covered the topics where we've had the most experience. For example, in addition to writing the introductions for Parts 1 and 2, I've talked about mental health, drawing on my wealth of experience as a child psychologist. Meanwhile, Sharon's experience as a teacher makes her the perfect person to cover aspects like the practicalities of starting secondary school and particular study techniques.

Between us, we agree on the key aspects we believe parents should be across. Firstly, both of us are really worried about the mental health of our early adolescents. Recent research by Hiscock, Neely, Lei and Freed in 2018 shows that a staggering 1 in every 7 young people (aged 0–19) has a mental illness, most commonly anxiety or depression. The rate of self-harm among this population has doubled over the past ten years, while presentations to accident and emergency for mental illness have tripled. All is not well for the early adolescent.

Secondly, virtually every psychologist I know thinks that the transition from primary to secondary school can be one of the toughest times in a child's life. It is unfortunate that starting secondary school occurs at a time when many young people are not only going through significant brain changes, but also dealing with the physical changes of puberty, which can be really confusing and challenging.

Thirdly, both of us believe in the power of practical, hands-on parenting. So much of great parenting is just showing up and being informed. The most exciting thing about this book is that we get to list the myriad things that parents can do to ease the school transition, build resilience and lay the foundations for a great journey through adolescence.

For example, some young people may need extra help with organisation and time management during this adjustment to the academic rigours of secondary school. Some parents may need to adjust their expectations of their child around the nature and extent of household chores at the start of the school year. Some students in particular become psychologically entrenched in the predictable, familiar routine of primary school and, when confronted with so many changes to that routine, can struggle to make the necessary adjustments.

Parents need to have a 'developmental perspective' (which we will explain) and display stratospheric levels of patience and understanding as their Year 7 student encounters things that are strange and different.

The main message of our book is that the secret to a great start to secondary school lies in planning, and in having a specific set of skills, knowledge and strategies for a successful transition into Year 7. We both believe that nothing is more important than your Year 7 feeling safe, valued and listened to as they transition into secondary school.

The good news is that you now hold in your hand my own experience, with over thirty years as an adolescent psychologist helping young people manage the stress and anxiety often associated with this period of their lives. You also have the expertise of Sharon Witt, who has taught secondary students for almost three decades and is experienced in helping young people navigate and experience success in secondary school. Between us, we have written some thirty books to help parents, children and teens navigate various stages of life and their associated challenges. What is amazing is that we both agree that this is the most necessary book yet.

Over the course of this book, we are going to arm you with information, stories and strategies to assist you in providing a safety net for your child as they enter the unfamiliar territory of secondary school. You will know what to expect, what you can do if you or your child are worried about a specific situation, and how to handle things like bullying, homework and friendship issues.

We want to give you and your child the best opportunity to thrive in secondary school. It is our hope that by the end of this book, you're going to feel a whole lot more capable of dealing with anything that Year 7 throws at you and your child.

The journey begins here

The experience of secondary school is different for everyone. Your son or daughter is made up of twenty-three chromosomes from you and twenty-three from the person that you made them with. Throw in the genetic roll of the dice, their environment and upbringing and you get a personality, disposition and temperament that is unique to your Year 7 (not a carbon copy of you).

As a result of this magical mix, for some (very few), the transition to secondary school is a breeze. We know quite a bit about these students and they tend to have the following characteristics:

- Impressive social skills
- Easy temperament
- At least average intelligence
- Attachment to family
- Independence
- Good problem-solving skills

But for most teens, this transition takes adjustment. As they move into Year 7, your child will have a lot to handle in a short space of time.

Is it fun? Yes. All the time? No. But can it be fulfilling? Absolutely!

The great news is that surviving and thriving in secondary school years is possible. Parents need to remember the golden rule in psychology: if you cannot change something, you can always change the way you think about it.

So there are two ways your child can approach the transition to Year 7: in OMG mode (catastrophising, awfulising, 'it's going to be terrible', etc.); or alternatively, thinking of it as a strategy game where they (and you!) need to equip themselves with the key competencies (inside knowledge) that will make this journey amazing.

We always take great care to express to Year 7 students the importance of putting the whole year into a broader perspective. The words we always choose to get this point across are some that we think should be on parental repeat throughout the first year of secondary school, as it's a vital message that can be reinforced at home:

'Many millions of people have indeed not only survived but have thrived through secondary school over the years! They have come out the other end better prepared for life, and have made some awesome friends along the way. You will be okay.'

Remember, secondary school is not the be all and end all. In Australia, you've got to go, it's compulsory, so go ahead and give the experience your best.

Most students will spend a maximum of six years in secondary school (less if they leave early to begin an apprenticeship or work) so this will only be a very small percentage of their entire life. It may seem like a long time while it's happening, but before you can blink, your child will be out in the workforce and living life on a much larger scale. So be positive! Parental attitude is so important. Helping them with homework, discussing their experiences at school and your willing participation in school-based activities all indicate to your child that you are interested in and value their educational experience.

I have been teaching secondary school students for the best part of three decades, which I regard as an absolute privilege and great fun (most of the time). I have used my experience to inform the advice and stories in this book, which will help your child (and you) to get through these years.

Enjoy this book and enjoy guiding your child in this next stage of their lives.

Part 1

A new world: secondary school

THE ADOLESCENT BRAIN

As parents, you need to understand that a Year 7 brain is still a 'work in progress'. The average Year 7 has 100 billion brain cells and 1000 trillion connections. When rested, fed, exercised and hydrated this brain will work quite well, generating up to 23 watts in electricity every single day. However, that brain won't be all wired up until your child is in their mid-twenties.

Parents of Year 7 children need to understand and remember this – I call it adopting a 'perspective' – in order to stop them from pulling their hair out when their children do jaw-droppingly stupid things. Over the years I have had parents say hilarious things about their Year 7s:

- 'Some of my children drink from the fountain of knowledge; Harry only gargles.'
- 'At times, I think my son is depriving a village somewhere of an idiot.'
- 'It's hard to believe he beat out 1 000 000 other sperm.'

- 'If she were any less intelligent I'd have to water her twice a week.'

Brain maturation is also influenced by genetics, environment and personality, which is why a minority of Year 7s may have figured out that the next six years are about acquiring the skills for future economic independence. Others see it as a refined form of torture, invented purely to keep them out of the house during the daytime. This is why one of the most common questions that parents have hurled at them in the lead-up to Year 7 is, 'What is the point of secondary school?' It's a good question, and one that is often asked by exasperated and stressed-out students across the nation.

ENCOURAGING YOUR CHILD'S OUTLOOK

While most adults reading this book understand the importance of secondary school, it's vital that adult carers realise that young people going into Year 7 may not see the value of their schooling until they themselves are adults. Parental attitudes, values and beliefs about Year 7, and secondary school in general, can help students gain a different view and actively enjoy their time in secondary school. So what are the key messages that parents need to relay?

Relationships are key

There is a consensus among most developmental psychologists that one of the greatest predictors of wellbeing in young people is having a wide range of friends. One of the benefits of secondary school is that your child will get the chance to learn to relate to a variety of different people and personalities, both in their own age group and with adults (like teachers, for example). These vital social skills will be extremely helpful to them when they go into university or the workforce. In that adult world, they will need the ability to relate to a wide range of people.

A crucial role for adult carers is to help prepare their Year 7s for the challenge of obtaining, maintaining and retaining friendships. Positive friendships are an important part of the secondary school journey. A positive friend is someone who walks the talk, and shows that they care through their actions – big and small. Positive friends help students discover important social and emotional skills, like being sensitive to other people's thoughts, feelings and wellbeing.

For teenagers going into Year 7, good friends can be like an individual peer support group. Friends and friendships give early adolescents a sense of meaning, purpose and belonging, a feeling of being valued that can help with developing confidence and a sense of identity. A positive peer group not only provides a way to experiment with different values, roles and ideas, it can also provide experience in getting along with people of the opposite sex (if in a co-educational setting; more about that on page 17).

Michael's definition of a good friend is someone who:

- is there for you, irrespective of the circumstances
- is not judgemental
- is not sarcastic or condescending
- does not put you down or deliberately hurt your feelings
- is always sympathetic, generous and respectful
- you like spending time with and whose company you enjoy
- is devoted, reliable and dependable
- will confront you when you are wrong
- makes you laugh and smile
- will listen and comfort you when you are upset

A major task for parents during Year 7 is to encourage as many positive friendship (not the local drug dealers, or outlaw motorcycle gang) relationships in and outside of school as possible. So ensure that you encourage your child to have friends over, create a welcoming space in your home, or just give your child's friends a lift home after social outings. It's amazing what you can learn in the space of a ten-minute car trip. This also shows your child that you understand how important these friendships are to them.

This does not mean that your child should be expected to like everyone – that would be boring and it's not even possible. But getting along with people takes basic social and emotional competencies, like tolerance, conflict resolution, anger management and problem solving. In short, while they do not need to be friends with everyone they meet, they do need to learn to cope with other people beyond a handshake or nod of the head. It isn't always easy, but this can be one of the best lessons learned during their secondary school years.

See tasks through

Another benefit that can come from secondary school is learning the value of commitment – finishing something once it is started – which is a key component of resilience. This might be learning an instrument, participating in a school play, completing a Science research assignment or attending a school sports carnival and running the 1500 metre race, even when they don't feel like it. Maybe they joined Student Council at the beginning of the year, and no longer feel like giving up their lunchtime once a week. Maybe they were really excited about learning guitar until they realised the amount of practice required to master it; maybe they joined the local swim squad but don't like getting up early; maybe they signed up for a drama production but want to pull out when they get a non-speaking part. Parents need to ensure that once a commitment is made, your child maintains that commitment through to the end (unless there are extreme extenuating circumstances). This demonstrates true character, and it will teach your Year 7 that they are capable of maintaining a commitment, even when they don't feel like participating.

Get organised

Learning to be an organised person during secondary school is perhaps one of the major benefits of school life. With greater responsibility expected from Year 7 and extending through to the secondary years, your child will need to develop their own organisational habits – what works best for them so that they can complete their necessary tasks, such as homework, study and completing assignments.

Many of these organisational skills – time management, study skills, presentation of work and completing assignments – will prepare students well for university or working in an environment where these basic skills are required. Whether they enter a trade or go on to university or enter the workforce straight from secondary school, basic organisation skills will be expected. (For more information on how to get organised, see page 134.)

'The classroom should be an entrance into the world, not an escape from it.'
—*John Ciardi*

THE STRUCTURE OF SECONDARY SCHOOL

Before I dive into the tools you need to help your Year 7 cope with secondary school, it is useful to take a look at the way schools are structured in Australia and the different kinds of school options open to your family.

There are a multitude of types and styles of secondary schools, just as there are many different personalities and needs of early adolescents. According to the Australian Bureau of Statistics, in 2017 there were 9 444 schools with 3 849 225 students enrolled in them.

It's important to note that whether your Year 7 attends a private or a public secondary school, they should still have the same opportunities available to any other student. School can be anything and everything they make of it, and it's up to them to seize whatever opportunities are presented to them. Parents should encourage their child to make the most of these opportunities, such as joining the school choir, debate team, basketball team, music ensemble or drama production. While your child might be resistant to stepping out of their comfort zone and trying something unfamiliar, particularly if older students are involved, the more they give things a try, the more their confidence will grow.

Public schools

Public secondary schools are basically run by government departments. The government decides what is taught and what facilities are available at the school. Public schools rely on taxes to provide much-needed funds to keep the school running. Generally speaking, Year 7 students are most likely to attend a public secondary school close to where they live, as students are usually allocated to public schools by location, or 'zones'. Sometimes parents can apply to a public secondary school that is out of their immediate catchment zone, especially if it has a specific program that is not offered in their closest school, for example a special sports or drama program.

Most public secondary schools offer excellent facilities and subject areas. There is no reason your child cannot receive the best education available in a public school. Many public schools get better results than prestigious, expensive private schools.

Technical or trade training schools

A number of years ago, the Federal government introduced funding into secondary schools across Australia to establish trade training campuses. Some schools created a technical arm of their existing school, while others went into partnership with local TAFE organisations to offer training for those students who wished to follow a pathway into a trade. There are also some independent trade training schools that were established under this new funding;

those schools may incur student fees. Trade training schools focus on more hands-on subjects such as carpentry, metal work and hospitality, while there are some secondary schools that have a more specific focus on sports or arts, such as drama and music.

Private schools

Private secondary schools are funded differently from public secondary schools, and generally rely on school fees that are paid by parents, with some additional government funding. School fees help to pay teachers' wages, provide school materials and facilities, and cover all the other expenses that come with running a secondary school. Some private school fees can be quite high, but that doesn't always make them the best school. One Sydney private school charged parents $38 000 a year in 2018. Wow!

Some private schools actually run from the first year (for example, 'prep', otherwise known as reception or foundation) right up to Year 12, or the final year of secondary school. If your child is attending a school such as this, they may be on the same site for both the primary and secondary stages. That certainly makes things easier when graduating from Year 6 – as does having a settled peer group and friendships.

On the other hand, a change of school can offer an opportunity for your child to experience a fresh beginning with social groups, which could be particularly helpful if they experienced issues in primary school.

Programs, subjects and resources may be quite similar across public and private schools, so school choice can often come down to a personal decision by parents and students. For example, some private secondary schools run specifically religious-based programs, which might best suit a family's core religious beliefs and values.

Same-sex and co-educational schools

Some secondary schools are structured as same-sex schools. That means it's an all-girls or all-boys school. For some adolescents, this works better, as it avoids the distraction of having students of the opposite sex in their classes. It also means that the school can be more flexible in the curriculum when offering courses that cater specifically for the one sex. According to Loren Bridge, the Executive Officer of the Alliance of Girls' Schools Australasia, young women at single-sex schools behave more competitively than their co-educational counterparts. Bridge claims that they are more assertive, more likely to take healthy risks, are more questioning, and engage in sport and physical education with increased frequency.

There is ongoing debate over whether girls and boys learn better separately. Some co-educational schools now teach core subjects like Maths, English and Science to single-sex classes. At the time of writing, the average scaled Australian Tertiary Admissions Ranking (ATAR) for girls in Year 12 is 78.70, and for boys is 68.35. Research shows that the majority of boys have been slipping behind girls in their learning outcomes for the past ten years. What is more, young men constitute only 43 per cent of enrolments in post-secondary institutions.

There is much debate among parents as to whether sending their young boy or girl to a co-educational school will be fraught with challenges once those raging hormones rear their ugly heads, usually somewhere in the middle of Year 8. They worry that their child will suddenly become so boy or girl crazy that all concentration at school will go out the window and it will be a downward spiral from then on. It is true that this hormonal shift coincides with this stage of life, however, there can be great advantages to going through secondary school with mixed sexes. Importantly, it mimics the real world – when young people enter university and the workforce, they will be negotiating with the opposite sex. Both girls and boys learn in a myriad of ways and have great influence on one another. Secondary school is a pivotal time for young people to learn to relate to the opposite sex in a safe and healthy environment, where teachers and parents can step in if and when issues arise. This also exposes students to different roles, and can help break down stereotypes. A co-ed school provides an environment where students of all genders have the opportunity to express themselves and share their views, which will teach them about equality and to explore each other's perspectives. At this important stage of early adolescent development, being in an environment with the opposite sex each day can also encourage the development of healthy self-esteem. By learning in a co-educational environment, boys and girls nurture mutual respect and empathy for each other. Students appreciate their own individual worth as well as each other's. By studying together, students collaborate in ways that enable them to rejoice in their differences as well as their similarities.

What the students have to say . . .

As someone who grew up in a family with only sisters, having a chance to grow up and experience life with the opposite sex (through my schooling) at a co-ed school was hugely beneficial. Learning how to relate to boys, how to talk to boys and see life through their eyes prepared me for my future relationships with men.

Lucy

I attended two separate co-educational schools during my secondary years. For me, it was a great experience to interact with both sexes as we learned to navigate teenage-hood. One of the things I appreciated most about this experience was that I learned to interact with guys as friends and co-students in a non-threatening environment.

Kate

I went to an all-girls school for my secondary schooling. It was a lovely school and as I was boy crazy, the single-sex school was good for me as I didn't have the additional distraction of the opposite sex to contend with. Because I had lots of boys around – through church, friends etc. – I never felt uncomfortable around boys. It was a fantastic school that encouraged girls to do anything.

Simone

I attended a co-educational secondary school. Attending a co-ed school helped in many ways including speaking with, working and learning about the opposite sex. It gave me the ability to learn how females should be treated and also taught me to be able to speak up when they weren't being treated properly (or when as males, we were also not spoken to appropriately). I personally feel that it allowed me to mature more quickly than I would have in an all-male school, as the peer pressure and 'jock mentality' is somehow created within all-male groups (I've seen this happen through my experience with sport teams).

David

When I think back about my secondary school experience in a Catholic co-ed school, I think it made me more receptive to changes in society and diversity in employment. At school I felt we were treated as equals, for example in the senior leadership group where I was the dual College Captain with a female. Our friendship groups were made up of boys and girls and some of our closest friends were of the opposite sex. We had the opportunity to experience relationships with each other through our secondary years surrounded by our peers and teachers. We all interacted together and socialised together, both in and out of school. We experienced friendship tensions and breakdowns together and, no matter who you were, there was always perspective from the opposite sex to support and assist you along the way. It was just the norm to us and due to that co-education format we are now more open, and leading the changes in society.

Tim

Interestingly, in 2019 the media excitedly reported a new study that suggested that girls who might otherwise be at risk of becoming less confident than boys may have higher self-esteem if they attend a same-sex school. Dr Terry Fitzsimmons, who led the study from the University of Queensland, found that from as young as six, some girls began to believe they could not be as clever as boys. The study found that girls who attended single-sex schools did not exhibit this crisis of confidence.

The researchers observed more than 100 000 students aged 12–17 in single-sex schools and found no significant difference between the self-confidence of boys and girls. Numerous previous studies have found that girls are less confident in their own abilities than boys, and this lack of confidence has been linked to the lack of women in science and technology careers. However, these latest results suggest that girls who are kept separate from the opposite sex may not start to believe they are inferior. Food for thought! Of course, research is one thing, but experience tells us that some young people will thrive in whatever environment they are placed in and that it really comes down to the unique psychological characteristics of the individual.

But wherever your Year 7 ends up attending secondary school, just remember – their experience will be theirs, and entirely dependent on what they make of it and the opportunities that they take. Whichever school they attend, or will attend in the future, it is important to stress to them that they should use this experience to their benefit and make the most of it!

CHANGES, CHANGES AND MORE CHANGES

'I am always ready to learn although I do not always like being taught.'
—*Winston Churchill*

Change can be tough. Certainly the time when students leave primary school for secondary school is filled with many transitions. Parents who anticipate these changes and discuss and deal with them before they are encountered can help make life much easier for their children.

Some of the most obvious changes students will face day to day include the set-up, or structure, of their classes. In primary school, they will have generally had one class teacher who taught them for the majority of the time. That one teacher was basically in charge of their schoolwork and helped them settle into class. They checked your child's homework, marked their work, wrote their reports, talked to guardians when necessary, helped them sort out friendship battles and maybe even offered some friendly advice. When the chemistry is right this teacher can be viewed by a student as a 'charismatic adult' (see page 113), a safe adult ally, or what my friend and colleague Maggie Dent refers to as a 'lighthouse' – a positive adult who helps support them when things get tough.

One of the biggest practical changes your child will face in secondary school is that they will instantly have more teachers. In fact, they are going to meet with a different teacher for each subject. Each will have a different teaching style on a continuum from very strict through to very laid-back; the problem is that your child is not going to like all of them. A parent's job is to help them adjust to this. (We will discuss this further in Part 3, on page 142.)

Someone once said that a goal without a plan is just a wish. There is no doubt that getting the practical aspects right can lead to lower stress and an easier transition for all year 7s. As we said at the beginning, the secret to success in Year 7 is planning.

What the students have to say . . .

My experience going from primary school to Year 7 wasn't that bad. As I was going to a secondary school with no one from my primary school, I thought that it was going to be difficult to make friends and adjust to all the changes, but it wasn't. I made lots of friends quickly, and everyone was new coming in Year 7. The teachers were super nice and Year 7 was actually fun.

Ellie

Starting a new school is scary, let alone starting a new secondary school. It's extremely stressful. Of course everyone is different, but for me it was so scary. Making new friends, all the new secondary school stuff like timetables, different classes all over the school, and hormones, they're the worst. Teenager plus secondary school stress equals not fun.

Charlie

Luckily for me, I attended the same school from primary school before moving into Year 7. I had to learn quickly to be organised and keep my workbooks neat and tidy. This made it so much easier to find things in my locker, writing books and school diary. Organisation really is the key. There is also a lot more responsibility placed on you in secondary school from student leadership, travelling from one class to the next. Overall though, secondary school is great.

Charlotte

Teachers

Your new Year 7 student will most likely have a teacher assigned to their class or year level who is responsible for guiding them during the early weeks of transition. These people are critical and they are the ones to approach should your child experience any issues early on, or if you have any questions or concerns. This person may be known as the year level coordinator, homeroom teacher or pastoral care teacher. Whatever their title, make sure you identify who your 'go-to' teacher is so that you can get help when things become a bit confusing or overwhelming. Get their email address or a phone number for the school office and put it in your phone.

Emailing or calling your child's year level coordinator or pastoral care teacher with early concerns can be crucial in ensuring a smooth transition into secondary school. Teachers can only work with what they know, so if your child experiences any issues early on, or if you have key information relating to your child's educational needs that may assist staff working with your child, it is advisable to inform the most appropriate teacher. Don't assume that all relevant information pertaining to your child (primary school reports, education, paediatrician's reports etc.) has been passed on to teachers.

Ideally, each teacher will receive a detailed dossier on your child before they even commence their first class but the reality is, your child may be one of several hundred, or even a thousand, brand new Year 7 students in their school.

From a teacher's perspective, email is the first port of call. Expect a reply within forty-eight hours. If you don't receive a reply, it is worth sending a follow-up email. Teachers are indeed busy, however, communication with parents is also very important. Sometimes a simple piece of information from a parent regarding their child can make all the difference in the classroom.

Case study

Johnny finds speaking out in front of the class excruciatingly painful (to the point of throwing up) so his parents want to gently advise the teachers of this. It doesn't mean that Johnny will be exempt from ever giving an oral presentation; however, it may just mean that extra care could be given, guidance offered and options provided.

A sample email may look like this:

Dear Mr Reedman,

I am writing to discuss with you my son Johnny Thwaites (Year 7A) who is presently in your class for English.

You may or may not be aware that Johnny experiences crippling anxiety when it comes to presenting verbally in front of his peers. This has been the case for most of his primary school years, though recently there has been some improvement. Johnny struggles to the point where he often becomes ill leading up to and even during a presentation.

We continue to encourage Johnny to try and find ways of overcoming his anxiousness around talking in front of the class, such as having a big sleep the night before, taking deep breaths and making sure he is well prepared and has practised his talk.

At this stage he is still extremely stressed about his talk this Thursday for English class. We want you to be aware of this and also ask if you could offer some suggestions or alternatives to Johnny? Is it possible, for example, for him

> *to present his first oral presentation for secondary school to*
> *a smaller group of peers at lunchtime?*
>   *We look forward to your response.*
>   *Jack and Megan Thwaites*
>
> Without being too pushy, Johnny's parents have communicated
> with their child's particular subject teacher and outlined a
> brief history and some present concerns. This opens up the
> lines of communication, which will hopefully allow them to
> find an agreeable solution. Now they are all helping Johnny to
> complete his work requirement in a way that he can manage at
> this point in time.

How to know if your son or daughter is anxious

In my experience, one of the best ways of knowing whether your child has an anxiety issue that needs attention is by looking at whether it affects the way your child is leading their life. The main criteria for this is avoidance, and another is hesitance. If, after a few weeks of Year 7, your child starts skipping school or insisting they don't want to attend, and other issues such as bullying, a learning difficulty or having trouble making friends have been ruled out, then it is most likely that they are suffering from anxiety. Anxiety is thought to affect around one in ten children, which makes it a very common, if not the most common, childhood wellbeing issue. This can have a significant impact on their independence, academic achievements, and general quality of life. Parents who are concerned that their offspring is suffering from an anxiety disorder should contact their year level coordinator and let them know of their concern, ask them to monitor the situation and, if necessary, alert the student wellbeing team.

When communicating with your child it is crucial that you keep the lines of communication open so that you can discover what is going through their mind, what they actually think. A good way to attempt this is with the following model: observe, ask, listen, give information and encourage support.

Observing means simply noticing any significant changes in behaviour (sleeping, eating, socialising). Then ask – say something like 'I've noticed that you seem really tired lately, are you sleeping okay?' Listen carefully to the response, paraphrasing it back to the young person, so that they know they have been heard. Give information (without going into lecture mode) about the issue, for example, 'I know that not getting enough sleep can make concentrating at school really hard.' Next, encourage support – suggest that you both visit the family doctor and see if there are some suggestions that they can make to help.

What the students have to say . . .

Parents need to be there for their kids, make time to spend with them and listen to them if they need. Once you have heard what your teenager has to say, try to put yourself in their shoes. You need to make time to have fun and relax with your kids. Even just a couple of hours with just the two of you can help refresh their mind and bring their battery back up to full. Help them with their homework. This really made a difference to my Year 7. And always be there for your teenager.

Zoe

In 2007, Indiana University's High School Survey of Student Engagement surveyed 81 000 students in 110 high schools across 26 states. The top ten reasons young people gave for hating secondary school were:

1. Homework
2. Bullying
3. Getting up in the morning
4. It's just so boring
5. Grades
6. Annoying people
7. Mean teachers
8. Exams
9. Physical education
10. School lunch

Orientation

One of the questions I think all parents should ask their child prior to the commencement of Year 7 is, 'What are you most worried about going into secondary school?'

The answers are usually along the lines of, 'getting around the school', 'becoming lost', 'finding my way to Mr Smith's class' – that is, mostly about basic navigation at the beginning.

The good news here is that there are many other students in exactly the same boat as your child. Many students won't know where everything is when they kick off secondary school, or where they are supposed to be at each hour of the day. They are certainly not expected to know their way around the whole school from the very first moment, so let them know that and ensure they don't stress too much about this. Finding your way around can even be a way to talk to new people and make friends.

One of the first things Year 7 students will notice about their new school is the size of the place. Often, secondary school is much larger than what they are used to. Primary school was like a village. Now they've moved into a town! Instead of the same classroom for most subjects, there are now multiple rooms and more corridors to get lost in, at least in the first week of classes. But don't worry. They'll soon learn their way around and then it won't seem so scary. Attending orientation days will help, as will maps and apps.

Almost all secondary schools have at least one orientation day for new students starting their first year. In fact, some schools I know of actually have several scheduled orientation sessions so that the students have a few opportunities to get to know the school and the other students. Most schools also offer parent and student information evenings in the lead-up to the start of secondary school. They're a great idea, and they usually cover subjects like timetables, classes, homework and other school information. Occasionally the school will even invite special guest speakers. I recommend making the most of these kinds of sessions if they are offered by your school. Meet the teacher evening? Go along. Year 7 parent

social night? Attend. Year 7 information evening? Be there (even if you feel you may be swimming in information at this stage). By attending these kinds of events at your child's school, you are not only making the most of the support your school is offering you as a parent, you are also modelling for your child the importance of engaging with their new school community and grabbing all of the opportunities that are offered with both hands.

If you do happen to miss an important information evening, ensure that you make contact with the school and ask for key documents to be sent to you, or access the school's website to download the key information.

During orientation days new students will most likely meet many of their teachers and have a tour of the school grounds to familiarise themselves with where their classes will be held and what facilities are available. They might also receive useful information on these days about sporting or other groups they could join during secondary school. They also find out important transport information and get the lowdown on canteen menus and days of operation. It is said that all fear is the fear of the unknown; orientation days are a vital first step in making the unknown known.

All students should be given a map of the secondary school at some stage during the orientation process. Make sure they take the time to familiarise themselves with where their main classes are being held. It might also be helpful to use a highlighter pen to show where they need to be for each class. Classrooms are often named by their building block and then classroom number, e.g. C16 or D2. Students will soon work out which rooms and buildings they need to be in. It could also be useful for students to do a 'trial run' for getting between their classes. If there is some spare time on a day they are visiting their new secondary school, they could walk around their classrooms to find the best way to get between them.

Subjects

As well as having lessons run by different teachers in varying class-rooms, students will also find they need a separate folder and workbook for each subject, and they will also have many more text-books to keep organised. This may seem quite stressful at first, but there are many tips that we will share later in the book that will help students keep on top of all these books (see page 136).

Small fish, big bowl

Many adolescents are quite concerned by the change of status when beginning secondary school. After being the oldest group in the final year of primary school – the school leaders, part of the most expe-rienced group in the school – they feel like they go to the bottom of the pecking order again when entering the secondary-school level. There are five other year levels older than them now, and that can seem more than a little overwhelming. Your job as a parent is to acknowledge the reality of the 'big fish in a small pond to small fish in a big pond' scenario and then remind them that they are never alone, and that they will only be the new kids on the block for around eleven months. That time will really, really fly.

Homework

Finally, one of the biggest changes that many Year 7s experience (and that causes them stress before they even begin) is that of homework.

Yes, there is that dreaded word. We'll talk about this in more detail in Part 3 (see page 149), but homework is just a necessary part of secondary school that your child will face as they become a more responsible and mature student. This is despite a 2015 Victorian Government Parliamentary Inquiry into the approaches to homework in Victorian schools, which found that 'there is limited research and quantifiable evidence regarding the impact and effectiveness of homework to improve student attitudes to learning and student achievement'. In other words, no one is really sure that homework does anything positive, but for whatever reason it is still a requirement in most schools. Most students don't really begin to tackle homework until Year 7, and many find it a real struggle.

The best news of all is that the journey into secondary school doesn't have to be an insurmountable challenge that your Year 7 faces alone. In fact, with the inside knowledge and helpful tips contained in this book, parents will find they will be able to offer the help and guidance needed for their child to become more and more capable and independent as they progress through their secondary schooling.

Timetable

During orientation, your child should also receive a timetable for their different school subjects and teachers. This may be very perplexing but it is important not to freak out here.

When Year 7s first see their timetable with all the different subjects, times and room numbers, it can seem pretty overwhelming, not to mention confusing. But be assured that it doesn't take long before their timetable seems like second nature. Some secondary schools run their timetables on a two-week cycle, which means that week one is different from week two before the process repeats itself again. Other schools run with the same timetable each week. Subjects are usually taught in blocks known commonly as 'periods', or lessons, and run for between 40–70 minutes. All parents should keep a copy of the timetable on the fridge or somewhere visible at home – just in case.

It is also important to note that many schools are now upping the parental involvement by introducing online parenting portals. These new high-tech portals are usually quite simple for parents to navigate, and allow parents to log in to their own child's school timetable, see assignments that have been set, detentions given and results and grades for work requirements. These portals usually provide useful information, including your child's teachers and their relevant contact details. They also provide access to that all-important school calendar, so both students and parents can be prepared.

Uniform

Most secondary schools have a summer and winter uniform, plus a sports uniform. It's important to ensure your child has all the correct parts of their uniform well before you begin the new school year. Sometimes, schools will have a second-hand clothing option and a uniform shop that parents can purchase items from. Make sure they get their school shoes in the school holidays before they begin, so that they can wear them around home a bit to make sure they're comfortable. But it is also a well-known fact that many young people experience growth spurts over the school holidays, especially in the foot department, so don't buy them too early!

Transport

Some students use public transport to get to and from their secondary school, some for the very first time. If your child is using public transport to get to school, it would be a good idea to have a practice run or two during the school holidays. Depending on how secure they feel, parents can offer to accompany them or pick them up at the end of the ride. At the very least, parents and students should familiarise themselves with the bus timetable and make an extra copy to keep in their schoolbag or diary. Over the past four decades the proportion of students who are physically active every day has significantly dropped. According to the Bicycle Network, in the 1970s (when Michael Carr-Gregg was at school), eight out of ten students rode or walked to school, but today that number has plummeted to just two out of ten. Parents, when geographically possible, should encourage their Year 7s to ride or walk to school, as by doing so they contribute to their minimum physical activity requirement of sixty minutes per day (as recommended by the Australian Government Department of Health). As another benefit, the Bicycle Network also found that students who walk or ride to school are more focused and ready to learn compared to those who have been driven.

Prospectus

Most schools produce a prospectus for the first year of secondary school. Parents should be able to pick one up from the school office if they don't receive one as part of their enrolment package. You will most likely also find a copy of this prospectus on your school's website. These booklets provide a range of useful information about subjects, teachers, homework, camps, canteen, maps and school phone numbers. Year 7s will often be too busy to read through this material, so offer to go through it with them.

SECONDARY SCHOOL SUBJECTS

'I am indebted to my father for living, but to my teacher for living well.'
—*Alexander the Great*

One of the more obvious changes going from primary school to secondary school is the increased number of subjects that your Year 7 will study. Initially, they will probably find this daunting. If this is the case, it's worth pointing out to them that they have already been doing these subjects in various forms all throughout primary school, they just may not have realised it.

Think about this: during their primary school years, did they ever learn about volcanoes and how they worked? Maybe their teacher showed them how to construct a model of a volcano out of papier-mache. There might have been some bicarb soda used, plus a bit of vinegar to simulate lava. Guess what? They were actually having a lesson in science.

Get them to recall the time that they planted seeds into cotton wool, watered them and watched their seedlings grow, and tell them that this was biology! When they have been writing poems in class about spring time or writing a book report, that's all included in the subject of English.

What about learning the names of countries, or when they completed a project on Japan? They may have even cooked up some Japanese food and shared it with classmates. Well, this is a subject that is often labelled Geography or History in secondary school.

The whole point of rekindling these memories is to demonstrate to your Year 7 that they are already prepared for what's coming up in secondary school: Science, Geography, English. Your job as a parent of a newly-minted Year 7 is to help them connect the dots. Such connections can make the new subjects seem less scary. On top of this, it's important to stress that the students will be given help along the way to get them up to speed on the different concepts and skills they'll need.

FIRST DAY NERVES

'Take a deep breath, begin the day, knowing it will all be okay.'
—*Sharon Witt*

Now picture this: it's your Year 7's first day of secondary school. They start at a new school and they know absolutely no one, except

Case study

Lisa went to a private school in Melbourne where the kids went all the way from the beginning of primary school (called 'Prep' or 'Foundation' in Victoria) to Year 12. That meant most of the students in Year 7 had known each other since their early years. Lisa came from a local primary school and was the only student making the switch to this new school. All her other friends had gone either to the local high or technical school.

So there she was, the archetypal 'new kid on the block'. Fortunately, she had a lovely first-year teacher, Mrs Smith, who was very kind and really helped her year level settle in well from the beginning. This teacher helped set Lisa up for a successful first year in secondary school. She ensured that Lisa had a buddy to show her around the school grounds at recess, someone she could ask questions of if she was unsure about where a class was being held, and checked in to make sure she was coping with the change to her new school. By affirming, guiding and encouraging her, she helped make the transition a relatively smooth one.

maybe one guy from a local church youth group. Their shoulders are groaning under the weight of a ridiculously heavy schoolbag. The path to the gate is already packed with students who actually seem to know their way around. They reach the first corridor, drawing on vague memories from an orientation day last November.

They finally locate Room 7B. Other Year 7s are milling around, already best friends, it seems. Groups of chatting 12-year-olds, lots of friendships. Even a few teachers walk by and get in on the conversations.

But for your Year 7, it is just them, on their own.

Most kids are especially nervous about their very first day of secondary school. It's perfectly normal to feel a bit unsure about that all-important first day. They might feel a bit sick or squeamish or they may feel like they have a billion butterflies throwing a party in their stomach. So what can parents say to help deal with these first day jitters?

The trick is to get them to remember that they are not alone. Many hundreds of thousands of kids all over the world are feeling all the same things as they are on their very first day of secondary school. And they all survive – just like your child will!

There are two key themes in giving advice to Year 7s:

Theme 1: If in life you cannot change something, you can always change the way you think about it. All Year 7s will have moments of stress, disappointment and upset in the course of the transition to secondary school. How they respond to these challenges will have a big impact on their wellbeing. It is axiomatic that they cannot choose what happens to them, but they can choose their own attitude towards what transpires.

Theme 2: See life as it is, but focus on the good bits. Positive emotions – like happiness, appreciation, inspiration and satisfaction – are not just great at the time. Research by Frederickson in 1998 demonstrated that regularly experiencing positive emotions creates an 'upward spiral', serving to build our psychological resources. What does that mean for the Year 7s? They need to be realistic about the challenges that they'll face, but it helps to concentrate on the good aspects of Year 7 and see the glass as half full rather than half empty. Before they start school, ask them to look for three good things each day that they can discuss with you after school. There is even an app for that (it is called Three Good Things and is available on the Apple App Store or Google Play).

By the end of that very first day many students find that it wasn't nearly as bad as they'd expected. You see, our minds are very powerful things. The brain can expect the future to be horrible, blowing it out of proportion into something scary and debilitating. The real event, when you actually get there, is often not so bad. These initial negative thoughts are best thought of (and explained) by parents as a 'CFD' or a 'Crappy First Draft' – the cognitive version of a first draft of an assignment that needs to be re-written, re-drafted, re-worked and replaced.

Self-talk

The key to having a positive perspective is your child's 'self-talk'. Self-talk is basically their inner voice, the voice in their mind that says the things they don't necessarily say out loud. All young people have a private conversation in their head from the moment they get up in the morning until they go to bed at night. It is like their own personal radio station – YEAR7FM. The average Year 7 doesn't realise that this running commentary is going on in the background, but their self-talk can have a large bearing on their confidence. The effect can be good or bad depending on whether their self-talk is positive or negative.

Negative self-talk is any inner dialogue that may be limiting your Year 7's ability to believe in themselves and their own abilities, and reach their potential. Positive self-talk makes them feel good about themselves and the things that they confront as they make the transition. It's like having an optimistic voice in your head that always looks on the bright side. The latest research from Mount Sinai St Luke's Hospital, led by Professor Alan Rozanski, suggests that positive self talk leads to better outcomes, and is known to increase mental and physical wellbeing, in particular cardiovascular health.

The Year 7 parent's job is to help your child make the connection between their thoughts, feelings and behaviours. We need to dare our Year 7s to imagine a brighter first day, a better start-up week, an encouraging first year at secondary school. And we need to help them understand that telling themselves it'll be okay is one of the best first steps to take to ensure that things will actually be okay. Encourage positive self-talk statements such as:

- 'I'll find my way.'
- 'Someone will help me.'
- 'I'll work out my timetable.'
- 'My bag won't be so heavy tomorrow.'
- 'I am doing the best I can.'
- 'I can totally make it through this test.'
- 'I don't feel great right now, but things will get better.'
- 'I will give people the opportunity to get to know me.'

There are many ways you can help your Year 7 make the connection between thoughts and feelings. Check out some fact sheets from ReachOut, Australia's best young people's wellbeing website. (One called '5 things to remember when starting a new school' might be particularly helpful.) The more they work on improving their self-talk, the easier they will find it. It's kind of like practising an instrument or going to sports training: it won't be easy to start with, but they will get better at it with time. Get them to try the online program MoodGym. MoodGym is like an interactive self-help book to help young people learn and practise skills that can help to prevent and manage symptoms of depression and anxiety.

Encouraging young people to consider their own thinking is very helpful. In my experience, most Year 7s generally play their cards really close to their chest and are unlikely to discuss their feelings with their parents. The good news is that there are some great online tools and apps that can help, such as Whats Up, MoodKit, Mind Shift and CBT Thought Record Diary.

Thought processes

When your child's self-talk conversation is unhelpful or 'distorted' it can predispose the student to depression or anxiety. Parents of Year 7s should be listening for any patterns of negative self-talk. One of the most helpful discussions with Year 7s can revolve around helping them to recognise and challenge these thought distortions. This is the basis of cognitive behavioural therapy and is a useful skill to learn. This does take some maturity, and some Year 7s may struggle with the task. Some of the most common distorted thought processes experienced by Year 7s are described below.

Learned helplessness

This involves young people acting helpless and dependent so that their parents feel sympathetic and end up doing things for them – from finishing their homework to acting as their chauffeur. These Year 7s effectively teach their parents not to expect a whole lot from them.

For example, Sasha's history teacher set a term-long project on Ancient Greece at the start of the term, and suggested ways in which the students could manage their time so that they could finish the project by the end of the term. It's now the last week of term and Sasha is in her bedroom crying inconsolably because she has too much work left to do on the project. Her mother, seeing that all Sasha has completed so far is a very nicely coloured-in front page, starts to google useful references and jot down notes.

All or nothing thinking

Often young people think in absolutes – people, things or events are all good or bad, with no middle ground. They tend to pronounce judgement using general labels: 'She's dumb', 'He's a loser', or 'He's a nerd'. They will condemn others on the basis of a single occasion or encounter.

For example, Toby's parents were keen to have him broaden his interests, so they took him to a local martial arts studio to check out some of the classes on offer. He attended one class but then refused to return, saying that the school was 'lame' and he would never go back.

Catastrophising

Catastrophising magnifies and exaggerates the importance of events, anticipating how awful or unpleasant they will be. Here students constantly predict that negative things will happen, always overestimating the chance of a disaster. If they do suffer a setback, they will view it as part of a never-ending pattern of defeat.

For example, Naomi has an important test next week. Her parents know that she has studied hard for it, but Naomi is in a panic because she has convinced herself she will fail, that this will set the trend for both Year 11 and 12, and that she will probably die lonely and poor.

Negative focus

Here your child focuses on the negative, ignoring or misinterpreting the positive aspects of a situation or, indeed, the facts. They see only the weaknesses of those around them, and forget or ignore their strengths. If their parents do anything positive, they filter out and reject this and focus exclusively on the downside.

For example, Charlotte has been trying to lose weight. She was 'good' all last week, but yesterday she blew it and had a piece of cake for dessert. She feels like such a loser! She's convinced she can't do anything right. She has spent the day mulling over the fact that she shouldn't have eaten that piece of cake. She's decided to go off her diet and eat the rest of the cake, and all the chocolate in the pantry, then start the diet all over again tomorrow.

Jumping to conclusions

In this case, a Year 7 interprets things negatively, even if there are no definite facts. They begin predicting the future and take on the role of mind reader, constantly predicting that bad things will happen.

For example, imagine Tony is giving a speech in front of his Year 7 class. A girl towards the back of the classroom yawns, so Tony goes home convinced that it was a terrible speech and that the entire audience was bored.

Living by fixed rules

Young people tend to have fixed rules and unrealistic expectations, regularly using words like 'should', 'must' and 'can't'. This leads them to be constantly disappointed and angry with those in their orbit.

For example, Sophie is kept waiting at school when her mother gets stuck in traffic. Her mum's mobile battery has run out, so she can't ring Sophie to let her know she's running late. It starts to rain and with each passing second Sophie becomes increasingly tense and angry. 'Why am I left standing here? Why didn't Mum ring? She's always late. She'd never do this to my sister . . .'

In my experience, many Year 7 students are actually truly excited about beginning secondary school. The excitement of a whole new environment, new subjects, responsibilities and friends is something they are looking forward to and are ready to embrace. Make sure you help them harness this positivity and encourage it. Encourage them to start monitoring their self-talk and challenge any negative thoughts.

No matter what position they are in – whether they are a nervous wreck or insanely excited about the prospect of secondary school – early adolescents will listen to and absorb what their parents say, so drip feed these messages to them in the weeks leading up to that fateful first day. And just remember, their first day of secondary school only happens once, and it will go quicker than they can blink.

Michael's top four questions to counter negative chatter:

1. Take a reality check

   Is there any evidence for what I am thinking? Am I filtering out the positives?

2. Look for an alternative explanation

   What is another way to look at this?

3. Put things in perspective

   What's the worst thing that can happen?

4. Ask goal-directed questions

   Is this way of thinking helping me to achieve my goals?

Self-talk is the substrate of attitude

Our experiences are very strongly influenced by our attitude. As a professional (a teacher), I have to make a conscious effort each morning to have a positive attitude and a smile on my face. For example, I might have received some really difficult news the night before, had an issue with one of my own children or even just had a night of no sleep. Any of these issues could have a negative effect on my attitude at work the next day. Now, can you imagine what my day (and the day of my students) would be like if I had a negative attitude towards being at work? What would it be like if I hated spending time each day with my students? Sometimes we have to 'fake it til we make it'. I may use self-talk such as, 'Today I choose to smile.' Or I might say to myself, 'Okay, I haven't slept, but today will be a great day. I am grateful that I have a job that I love and students that I appreciate.' This doesn't mean that I don't sometimes let my students know that I didn't sleep well the night before, or am fighting off a cold – being honest often helps within the classroom.

But our attitude – how we act and behave in front of others – can have a large impact on our experiences at school.

It is crucial that your Year 7 understands that no one else but them can control their attitude. Let's say they are given an assignment and their first thought is, 'What a stupid assignment. How boring!' Well, you can bet that they will drag their feet to get that assignment finished, if at all. And it probably won't be their best work.

If your Year 7 is just about to begin secondary school and their attitude towards school has always been pretty poor, do you think things will be any better in secondary school? There is an old saying that the greatest predictor of future behaviour is past behaviour. Given that behaviour is often an expression of attitude, the odds are probably not with you if they have the same old attitude. I often say to the young people I work with, 'No matter what your attitude was in primary school, and no matter what subjects you struggled with, you can change your attitude right now. And believe me, secondary school will be different because you have a choice to totally change your attitude.'

The ability to control our own attitude is a unique and precious gift. Sure, bad days will happen and things will go wrong, but we always have a choice about how we will react to these things.

Parents can encourage incipient Year 7s to be positive about the new experiences. Stress that our past experiences don't define what our new experiences will be, but that they do need to have an attitude – and it should be a good one!

One of the problems is the word itself. The way we use 'attitude' nowadays ('She's got an attitude' or 'He's got an attitude problem') is always clouded in negativity. The truth is, a good attitude is just as powerful as a negative one. An 'attitude' is quite simply a state of mind – how to think and act. So you should encourage your child to have a positive, 'I can do it' attitude! It's not the circumstances and problems that we encounter (and you'll encounter many, that's for certain) that shape our lives. It's our attitude and how we respond that really matters.

I really admire the example set by a guy named Justin Herald.

He was an ordinary young man who, by his own account, didn't do too well in school. Some of his teachers complained to him that he had an attitude problem. One teacher in particular, Justin recalls, told him that he wouldn't get anywhere in life (or words to that effect) and that he would probably end up dead or living on the streets.

Well, as the story goes (and it's a true story), Justin Herald did have an attitude problem. As a young guy, with only $50 in his bank account, he decided to use his attitude problem for the better, and came up with some attitude slogans. Phrases such as 'If I want your opinion, I'll ask for it!'

With his small amount of cash, he organised the purchase of some T-shirts and screen-printed his attitude slogans on the front of them. Before long, Attitude Inc was formed. People purchased his new attitude T-shirts by the truckload. Before Justin knew it, he had used his attitude to begin a multi-million-dollar business that is still thriving today, all because Justin was determined not to let one negative voice from one teacher determine his future success.

Justin has often shared the story of how he was at one of the clothing stores near where he lived, which stocked his T-shirts. Out the front of the store, he bumped into the teacher who had openly bagged him in secondary school.

The teacher said: 'Ah, Justin Herald. I'm surprised to see you still alive! I knew you wouldn't get anywhere in life.'

Justin just bit his lip and smiled. Because that teacher was actually wearing one of Justin's shirts – and he had no idea that Justin's successful company produced them!

You see, it's all about attitude!

Parents need to send a message to their children in no uncertain terms: 'Don't ever let anyone tell you that you can't achieve something, or that you are hopeless. You are not! People who feel the need to give a negative opinion or want to cut you down when you share your hopes and dreams have no business trying to put their bad attitude on to you. Instead, take that attitude to drive you to succeed in whatever you choose to do with your life.'

TAKEAWAYS FROM THIS SECTION

- Set the scene for success
  Ensure that your child has all the books, uniform and resources they require to begin secondary school in an organised and positive way.

- Reassurance
  Reassure your child that they have a positive framework around their entry into secondary school and that they have lots of support in place.

- Communication

  Communication is key. Ensure that you make time to talk with and listen to your child as they take on this new and often scary stage of their schooling. Remember to communicate any concerns regarding your child to their year level coordinator or pastoral care teacher.

- Patience

  Remember that your secondary schooler's brain is a work in progress, and as such, they may require lots of visual and verbal reminders, as well as patience, as they settle into a new environment and routine.

- Self-talk

  Parents need to remind their Year 7s that the way the student talks to and feels about themselves is the key to learning how to be more positive. Thinking negatively is really just a bad habit that they can unlearn.

Part 2

Getting right on the inside

As parents, the pre-teenage and teenage years sound more than a little scary: contending with issues such as cyber bullying, stress, drugs and sex. With so many horror stories and negative statistics in the news, it's understandable for parents to feel overwhelmed, anxious and helpless. But apart from crossing your fingers and hoping for the best, there are some other things parents can do to help their children through early adolescence.

Early adolescence represents an important stage in young people's development. Important experiences such as making friends, figuring out who they are, emancipating from adult carers and genuinely engaging in learning can all have a significant and enduring impact on each Year 7 student.

Although adolescence does involve Year 7s stepping out from the shadow of childhood and breaking some of the emotional bonds that bind them to their adult carers, it is also useful to understand this as a time when adults and Year 7s are trying to work together. All parties need to navigate a change in the relationship that seeks to balance a desire for independence with maintaining an ongoing relationship. The emphasis on each aspect depends in part on the individual psychology of the adults, their experience of being parented, and their religious and cultural background.

Early adolescence is the first stage of adolescence and occurs from ages 10 to 14. Puberty usually begins during this stage. Young people in early adolescence become acutely aware of their changing bodies and often start to worry about their physical appearance. They might experience shyness, blushing, modesty, and a greater interest in privacy. A key question they may have is, 'Am I normal?'

Such worries are intensified by the marked variations in development at this age. Within the same Year 7 class will be 13-year-old boys with squeaky voices and fully mature teens who look like full-grown men. Similarly, physically immature girls who have yet to experience their first menstrual cycle are mingling with fully developed counterparts who could pass for women several years older.

Early adolescents may feel ten feet tall and bulletproof and start to engage in risky behaviours such as smoking and alcohol use. This period may also be characterised by sexual curiosity, which is usually expressed through admiration of celebrities, singers, and actors. These broader behavioural challenges sit alongside the experience of starting Year 7 and can complicate the transitional period. The teenage brain is undergoing some key changes at this time; it is as if a neurological veil is lifted and the young people look at their parents for the first time through adult eyes. They start to realise that their parents are not infallible and begin to identify their faults. It is also common for early adolescents to show acting-out behaviours. They seek out novelty and risk, are not very good at reading emotions, are heavily susceptible to peer pressure, have trouble regulating their emotions, and struggle to get enough sleep. The attitudes of early adolescents to their adult carers aid their emancipation: they often start to regard adult carers as embarrassing or old-fashioned. The desire to be with mates their own age rises and the parental cringe factor with some Year 7s can be quite high. The way in which parents respond to the growing independence of Year 7s and their own temporary obsolescence is critical. It is difficult to understate the importance of maintaining a developmental perspective and leaving the lines of communication open.

The trick is to make time during the day or evening to hear about your teen's activities; be sure that they know you are actively interested and listening carefully. Remember to talk with your teen, not at them. Ask questions that go beyond 'yes' or 'no' answers to prompt more developed conversation. Take advantage of time during car trips to talk with your teen. Try not to miss sporting and school events, and make time to play games and talk about current events.

One of the biggest mistakes that Year 7 parents make is not giving their children enough Vitamin 'N' (saying no to unreasonable requests) and failing to set limits and boundaries about things that relate to their wellbeing. Parents should avoid trying to appease Year 7s by giving them everything they want, and let them experience adversity.

Year 7s thrive when the family has fixed and regular rituals and traditions, when they are kept busy with sport, art, music, dance and drama, and when parents keep a close eye on who they are hanging out with. If you want to know how your Year 7 is going, check out their peers.

So how do you know if things are not going well with your neurotypical Year 7? The four key components* to watch are:

- Do they have friends?
- Can they manage to be away from you? (e.g. school camps, sleepovers etc.)
- Do they have hobbies that they enjoy?
- Do they attend school regularly?

The key strategies for the parents of Year 7s should be:

- Keep calm
- Don't talk too much – listen more
- Look for compromise and negotiate
- Use humour
- Set very clear boundaries
- Avoid confrontations or ultimatums
- Only argue over things that matter
- Do not constantly remind them of past mistakes
- Talk while doing something together
- Let some things go

* Any problem in these aspects of their life should be cause for alarm and warrant a chat with the school welfare person.

IT'S OKAY TO MAKE MISTAKES

'Fall seven times, stand up eight.'
—*Japanese proverb*

As previously discussed, the Year 7 brain is not wired up yet and therefore Years 7s are more likely to take risks and seek out novelty. They are not great at reading emotions, they are more susceptible to peer pressure and exhibit less self control. In taking the developmental perspective, outlined in Part 1 (see page 9), we need to remember that they will make errors of judgement, forget stuff, get emotional and yell from time to time. As far as school is concerned, the part of the brain that controls motivation – the right ventral striatum, in medical jargon – is so poorly developed in teenagers that even getting out of bed in the morning is a major challenge.

Throughout their secondary school years (and beyond!), your Year 7 will make mistakes – that's a given. These may include some risk-taking mistakes on social media, such as oversharing

> Michael's rule:
>
> When you tell a Year 7 student something:
> - Tell them you are going to tell them something important.
> - Tell them.
> - Tell them what you just told them.

information about themselves or sharing inappropriate images, losing valuable items (phones, clothes, shoes), misuse of technology, skipping school and early risk-taking behaviours.

It's important as parents to reassure your secondary schooler that, despite the fact that they will make mistakes along the way, nothing is ever so bad that they cannot come to you or another trusted adult and work it out together.

Let's say your secondary schooler gets a test back from their teacher. They realise that they didn't pass the test. It's not surprising, as they didn't actually study for it. Their teacher tells them that they are more than capable of passing this test as they know how to solve the problems – they just hadn't practised! So now they've got a plan for next time. Study. Practise. And be prepared ahead of the test rather than worrying about it as they walk into the classroom to actually take the exam.

It's not always a bad thing to fail or make a mistake. If they learn their lesson from the failure, that's the main thing.

Thomas Edison made many hundreds of mistakes, or failures, before he finally invented a functioning filament in a working light globe. Rather than giving up after the 100th or even 300th try, he remained determined. He knew that eventually he would find success . . . and he did!

Something that has become increasingly obvious in the past decade is the rise in young people who are concerned with failure. It is concerning that many students will enter secondary school with a negative mindset about not being good enough. They may have really struggled with maths or spelling during their primary school years, thus already setting their mindset for perceived future failures.

When I begin the new year with a fresh bunch of English students, one of the very first things I do is ask them what aspects of English they struggle with the most. For example, which students really struggle with spelling? I identify the students who have difficulty reading a novel, and those who find writing a chore. I then ask them to reframe these supposed areas of struggle, and focus on the things they can do, rather than the issues they feel have held them back previously. If they struggle with spelling, I encourage them to write freely regardless, and I will work through the spelling by editing later. If reading has always been an issue, I will look into audio recordings of the novel and also spend time in class reading the novel together. It's important that your Year 7 doesn't go into the new school year focused on making mistakes.

As parents, you have to understand that, despite their best intentions, your child, by the very nature of being human, will make mistakes at some point. Or they will find themselves in a situation that upsets them or concerns them greatly (e.g. being bullied, receiving an unwanted request for a naked image, being the subject of cruel gossip etc.).

We should remind our children that they can come to us with *any* concern and reassure them that, although we may feel disappointed, we will not get angry or overreact, but will work through any issue any time.

When my own son was in primary school, he had been at a local football event one weekend and found a football belonging to the club in the long grass by the playground. He made the decision to take this football home. Before long, my son was so guilt ridden at being in possession of 'stolen property' that he woke me in the early hours one morning to 'come clean' over his 'crime'. In the mind of my 10-year-old son, he had made the worst mistake imaginable and half expected the local constabulary to beat our door down at any moment and arrest him for theft.

By reassuring my son that he could always come to me when mistakes were made, he did indeed talk to me when he needed to. On this occasion, I thanked him for approaching me and being honest. We were then able to devise a plan together – in this case we posted the football back to the local club in question.

Being consistent with my son when he has made a poor decision, and reassuring him that we will work through the solution together, meant that when he made other mistakes when he was older he still came to me to talk them through, so we could once again reach a solution together.

Parents: if you are faithful and show you can help solve small mistakes with your children, they are most likely to come to you when they make bigger mistakes. Mistakes are simply evidence that we are trying. We should be more concerned for the student who never makes mistakes because they continually play it safe, rather than risk pushing themselves to achieve more.

PERFECTIONISM

If your Year 7 student makes an error in their written work, do they simply rub it out and keep going, or do they become agitated, upset and frustrated and embark on a seemingly endless journey where they stay up all night, poring over it and 'polishing' it to perfection?

While there have always been high achievers at school in Year 7, both Michael and I have noticed a rise in the number of Year 7s who aspire to stratospherically high marks, brilliance in sports, art, music, dance and drama, exhausting themselves in the process. A minority will work themselves up into quite a state trying to hand in the 'perfect' assignment, and in so doing deprive themselves of sleep, miss out on the joy of learning and in some cases seriously compromise their health and wellbeing. Many teachers tell us that they are increasingly grappling with the rise of chronic perfectionistic thinking in their students. Around 1 in 7 primary and 1 in 4 secondary students display significant levels of anxiety (as measured by Beyond Blue in 2015 and Mission Australia in 2016, respectively). This perfectionistic thinking has been identified by Curran and Hill in a 2017 study as a risk factor for anxiety, depression and even eating disorders. In essence, more and more Year 7s seem

consumed by A-star expectations alongside a dread of failure. This is often fuelled by social media platforms like Snapchat and Instagram that lock our 13 and 14 year olds into a battle of mutually assured depression and anxiety. Some argue that social media is encouraging Year 7s to be more dissatisfied with their bodies, as well as pushing a message that this is modifiable. Researchers worry that Snapchat and Instagram are teaching Year 7s that how they look and what they wear are the most important things about them; that their sexuality is a currency and that the world is a scary, lonely, dangerous and competitive place.

One solution to this issue has been proposed by Oxford High School for Girls, which in August 2019 introduced a program called 'The death of Little Miss Perfect', aimed at stamping out perfectionism. It teaches students that it is 'fine not to get everything right', and submits students to online tests which become progressively harder within a time limit so that pupils are deliberately unable to answer them. The headmistress, Judith Carlisle, says, 'Real life is not about perfection. Even the most successful of lives has its share of setbacks, disappointments and failures.'

Multidimensional perfectionism (trying to be great at everything) can be extremely detrimental to the self-esteem of Year 7s. That is not to say that they shouldn't aspire to do well, but chronic perfectionism involves a lot of self-criticism and unless they can moderate that, they may become more susceptible to doing drastic things.

Dr Danielle Molnar, a psychologist at Brock University, Canada, argues that perfectionism should be considered as a risk factor for disease in the same way as obesity and smoking. In 2006

Dr Molnar studied 500 adults aged 24 to 35 who completed the 'Multi-Dimensional Perfectionism Scale', which measures perfectionistic tendencies. She found that socially-prescribed perfectionists (those who believe that others hold unrealistic expectations for their behaviour that can't be lived up to, and believe that others evaluate them critically) had worse physical health than non-perfectionists, made more visits to the doctor and took more sick days, so it would appear that nipping overly perfectionistic tendencies in our Year 7s in the bud may be a smart move.

FRIENDSHIPS

When we speak to young people about the reasons why they do or don't enjoy their secondary school experience, one of the most common responses has to do with friendships and social interactions. In fact, friends and peer groups are one of the highest priorities in the lives of most teenagers, and it makes sense that the bulk of these interactions occur at school.

Friendships built throughout your secondary school years can indeed be a lifelong and wonderful bond. But some young people really struggle with making friends. School can be a tough, isolating place and it can be lonely at times. If that's what it feels like for your child, and they really hate school due to friendship issues, be assured, they are not alone! There are many young people out there who struggle socially at school. I know that may not seem very reassuring right now, but there are some useful tips we'll look at in this book that may help your Year 7 expand their social network at school.

> **Case study**
>
> Annabelle was feeling disheartened about not having many friends in her year level in secondary school, and that nobody seemed to see that she was so alone. She'd even sat in a cubicle in the toilet block one lunchtime and complained later that no one had even noticed.
>
> Stepping back from the emotion she felt, the physical isolation she caused by locking herself in the cubicle was actually the problem. The truth is, she had been missed. People didn't know where she had gone but each assumed she was spending time with others. Annabelle really needed to get out and give other people a chance to be her friend.

All our children are worth getting to know and they have a great deal to offer other people – namely, their friendship. But they will often need to take the first step and give others the opportunity to get to know them.

Ralph Waldo Emerson once said, 'The only way to have a friend is to be one.' When you really stop and think about it, can your

WHY?...WHY?
WHY DOES NO-ONE WANT TO
PLAY WITH ME THIS RECESS??

Year 7 really expect to have great friends if they aren't willing to be one themselves?

Perhaps they are really shy, and that's okay. Some people are not very outgoing and we are not asking them to change their personality. But they will need to sometimes step out of their comfort zone and into their courage zone to take that first step to say hello to someone. As an educator, I often encourage my students to practise being friendly towards others. When we act in a friendly way – using eye contact, smiling and asking questions – we show that there is an opportunity to make a new friendship. You can assure your Year 7 that they will be pleasantly surprised once they start making conversation with others.

What students have to say . . .

My experience was not too bad moving into secondary school. After a few weeks I was fine and felt organised but it still felt like a very big leap from primary school. I had to learn a lot of new things. Making new friends seemed challenging because I didn't feel myself. Once I relaxed more, I began making friends.

Kiana

When I moved to secondary school, I basically had no friends at the start of the year. But I began to play basketball with people I didn't know, soon they became friends. In secondary school, you have to work hard. Things will begin to become difficult if you're not doing anything.

Jack

Secondary school is hard. Maybe even harder these days with all the pressure of social media. There is all the unneeded pressure to fit in and hide who you really are. Social changes impact you the most in secondary school. Sometimes, friends just get up and leave and it's sometimes really hard just to see your old friends hanging out with new friends. Social media just makes that easier to see.

Faith

In my first week of secondary school I reckon I probably said three words. I am a very shy person as it is but I found the first week of a new secondary school absolutely terrifying. Coming to a completely new place with new people was very nerve-racking. You've gone from being the oldest and biggest in primary school to the smallest and youngest in secondary school. My main tip would just be to be confident and try and talk to people, especially the ones who look exactly how you feel. I know it's really hard at first, and the first term of secondary school was probably the scariest time of my life, but give it time and you will be fine.

Ruby

The transition to Year 7 was difficult for me. I would be up late at night thinking about how I could make new friends, and how I could make people like me. I had never worried about making friends before secondary school started. I would stress over the smallest things and I kept thinking to myself, 'As soon as I make good friends and people like me, I'll be happy.' And I did; I made some awesome friends that I'm still friends with today. But I wasn't happy. I was continually judging myself: Oh no, they didn't want to be my partner, do they hate me? They haven't replied to my text, did I do something wrong? They didn't talk to me much today, I must be so annoying. I always thought they didn't like me, even though I knew that was wrong. It was like my brain wanted me to feel bad about myself. It was hard getting over that stage, and I'm still to this day not completely over it. But it's better than it was, and I just hope that nobody else questions who they are like I did.

Amber

Strategies to deal with shyness

Shyness, to some degree, can be considered normal among children, particularly when they find themselves in unfamiliar territory such as starting secondary school. It's quite normal for your child to feel they want to hold back a bit in new social situations. They may initially be unsure of what to say in front of new peers or worry about saying the wrong thing and making the wrong impression. So what can parents say to their young person on the cusp of Year 7 to help them emerge from the shadows of shyness?

Have realistic expectations

If your child has the goal of securing ten besties by the end of the first week of Year 7, they may be setting themselves up for disappointment. A more achievable goal might be to introduce themselves to just one new person in their first week. Encourage your Year 7 to set a realistic new friendship goal.

Recall the outstanding characteristics that they have

According to leaders of the positive psychology movement, such as Christopher Peterson and Martin Seligman, we each have twenty-four character strengths. Your Year 7 may be a bit shy, but that doesn't mean that they haven't got other assets. If they are self-conscious about being a bit of an introvert, remind them about all the other great skills they possess.

It's not about you

Year 7s who feel self-conscious often believe that other students are constantly evaluating them: what they say, how they look and what they do. This type of self-talk is not just unhelpful, it also has no basis in fact. Parents can play an important role in reminding their Year 7 that an objective examination of the facts would reveal that the other students are just busy getting on with their own lives and not judging others at all. In fact, if we could get inside their heads we'd see that the vast majority are totally consumed by their own issues.

Become a questioner

If your Year 7 finds themselves worrying about being judged by others, encourage them to change their focus to the other students. One of the all-time most effective strategies for shy students is to get them to ask other students questions about themselves, to learn more about them and develop an internal dossier on potential friends. Parents can help their Year 7s practise questions that they can ask fellow students to find out who is who in the Year 7 zoo.

Avoid avoidance

Most shy Year 7s tell me that they are reluctant to engage in any social situation; they say that it makes them feel anxious and awkward. Parents need to become a cheer squad, stressing that every time they have a go at socialising they will become better prepared to deal with it in a way that they enjoy. Parents can help their children by sharing ways to consciously overcome these feelings and using specific, evidence-based techniques. Start small and build up.

Techniques that parents can teach their Year 7s include:

- Slow breathing: a person's breathing rate increases automatically as part of the fight or flight response. Teaching your child to slow their breathing rate when they are anxious can settle some of the other anxious sensations, as well as help them to focus their mind. Try using the app Calm or ReachOut Breathe.

- Switching focus: swapping a Year 7's attention from themselves to a focus on others can go a long way towards diminishing social anxiety because they can't pay attention to two things at once. The more they focus on what's happening around them, the less they'll be affected by anxious thoughts.

- Support them: remind them to try to listen to what is really being said, not to their own negative thoughts.

- Focus: Urge your Year 7 to focus on the present moment, rather than worrying about what they are going to say or beating themselves up for a flub that's already passed.

- Release the pressure to be perfect: focus on being genuine and attentive – qualities that other people will appreciate.

What students have to say . . .

Transitioning into secondary school was probably one of the hardest things I have ever done. In primary school, I never paid too much attention to what the teachers were saying about Year 7 and I didn't think it would be a big issue. On my first day, I found it really difficult to talk to new people. None of my previous friends attended my new school and it was very intimidating. I never reached out to people and I thought they would approach me. If I could go back to my first day I would try to talk to new people. For people that are shy like me, I know it can be difficult but it is worth it.

Jamie

Since I came from a different primary school, I knew no one at my new secondary school. It was hard at first and you feel alone but a bit of advice is to try and find at least one friend that you can stick with and help you get around the school and as they gain more friends, so can you or vice versa. By doing that, you can be helped or you can help someone else. Try and be nice to teachers and not be disruptive in class.

Matt

Important qualities to look for in friends

'A friend is what the heart needs all the time.'
—*Henry Van Dyke*

Our experience in life tells us that friends will drift in and out of our children's lives. What's more important than how long a friendship lasts is that friends accept your Year 7 for who they actually are. Parents can play a useful role in emphasising that a good friend demonstrates that friendship in their actions, big and small.

Honesty

Good friends will always tell the truth, even if they know it's not necessarily what the other person wants to hear. Parents should encourage children to seek out this quality in their friends and to be able to trust and rely on the honesty of those they associate closely with. For example, if a friend invites them over for a Saturday evening one weekend, only to send a message that morning explaining that a family event has come up and they need to postpone, your Year 7 needs to feel confident that this is what has happened rather than become anxious that it is just a ploy to get out of their plans. A good friend needs to be trusted to speak the truth, rather than tell a fib because they have changed their mind.

Acceptance

True friends will accept your secondary schooler for themselves – they will love them because of who they are, for the good parts and the not-so-good parts, their unique personality, gifts and talents. Your child may also have the opportunity to make new friendships with others who find social situations difficult, or who experience shyness. Accepting others for their similarities as well as differences is a key element of friendship.

Shared interests

Friends often share passions and interests but also understand that they don't have to love everything the other person likes. In fact, having different interests actually provides a great opportunity to broaden each others' horizons. It helps if friends have some things in common, whether that is similar taste in films, music or sport, and these shared interests can encourage secondary schoolers to try other things their friends like.

Listening

Young people very often want to communicate with others, especially their closest friends. Good friends can be there just to listen if that's what is needed. Sometimes sharing a problem or some exciting news can make all the difference to your young person. Of course we hope that they will come to us if they need to discuss an issue that is concerning them, but sometimes opening up to a close friend of a similar age or stage can bring a fresh perspective.

Stickability

Good friends will always stick right by each other – if one is being bullied or has made a mistake (as we all do from time to time) a solid friend won't quit on your child. If you find that your young person seems to be making and breaking off friendships on a regular basis, it is worth exploring this with them. Perhaps there is an issue occurring that is making it difficult for your child to manage their friendships and keep them.

Kindness

I sometimes think our young people can forget the importance of simple, old-fashioned kindness. Without doubt, kindness counts for a lot in friendships. Not only is a good friend one who treats their friends well, it's also one who treats everyone with kindness. Secondary school can provide many opportunities to practise kindness towards others, without the expectation of anything in return. Simply asking someone to join in a group during recess or lunch or to join a team for a sport activity can make another person's day.

Humour

A sense of humour is not a prerequisite for engaging in friendship. However, it sure can go a long way when friends can have a good laugh together. There are many different types of humour, and finding someone who shares yours can be valuable. Most students I talk to about the qualities of robust and lasting friendships mention humour and the ability to laugh at similar things. Laughter can provide the ideal circuit breaker during some of the more stressful periods of secondary school.

Teaching Year 7s the characteristics of what it is to be a really good friend is essential. Ultimately, a friend will be someone who is there for your young person, no matter what, who will not be judgemental, will not put people down or deliberately hurt their feelings, will be kind and respectful, whose company we enjoy, and who will be loyal, trustworthy and willing to tell the truth, even when it's hard, will make them smile and comfort them when they are upset.

What students have to say . . .

I was from a completely different school with no friends, I didn't even know anyone going to my new school. I think in terms of finding friends I was lucky, I met a group of people that are still my friends now in Year 8. But some aren't as fortunate, some kids might get placed into a group of people that aren't good for them and it is difficult to find new friends after you have already joined a group. As much as being popular sounds nice, make sure to think of the consequences and the black hole of drama you are entering into. If you're searching for friends, find some that you are comfortable being yourself with because most likely you will be stuck with those friends for most of Year 7 and, if you like that friend group, then maybe the rest of secondary school.

Maggie

Moving from Year 6 into Year 7 was a fairly big change for me, coming from a different school. I would say try and make friends quickly, be organised and also be yourself. Don't pretend to be someone you are not.

Abby Grace

It can be hard taking that first small step into making a conversation with someone, someone you know nothing about and when you're clueless of how a relationship with that person will go. But it is so important to take that little step, be courageous and friendly and it will take you a long way. Know your surroundings and be observant – it will help you notice the people you would most likely fit in with.

Grace R

Managing friendships in Year 7 was stressful. With all the homework we were given, I had too much on my mind to realise that some of my friends weren't loyal. Because of this I am now dealing with a 'friend' who I can't really get rid of, and I am struggling to resist her mean actions. I wish that parents had more control over their kids, were able to guide them more onto the right path, enabling them to do good deeds instead of bad. Without my parents guiding me throughout secondary school, I'd be in such a mess.

Miranda

When a friendship is unhealthy

Unhealthy friendships can feel a bit like a vacuum cleaner, sucking all the energy out of you. They are the equivalent of a psychological black hole which just absorbs energy but gives nothing back. In other words, unhealthy friendships are one sided, that is, one person is always doing the work and having to help out the other one. It's all heading one way. While it is true that all great friendships will be tested at times, and will go through difficulties at certain points in life, parents have a role in reminding their Year 7 that a true friendship is a partnership and it needs to work for both parties.

Needy friends can be quite difficult, such as the friend who has a low self-image and is always complaining about being 'too fat' or 'too ugly'. You only hear from needy friends when they feel bad and they never really feel better, no matter how anyone tries to help. If you try to talk about yourself to a needy friend they don't seem to care, and yet they need constant reassurance that you like them. Needy friends often want to spend all their time with you, and they tend to dominate the conversation.

There is only a certain amount of this that people can take. But while these types of friends can drain your emotional energy, they are not necessarily completely toxic. My advice for young people here is simple: be a good friend. Affirm your friends, and remind them that they are important and worthwhile people. However, it is good advice for your child to be intentional about setting limits in how much time they spend with draining friends.

Sometimes friendships in Year 7 do not work out and can become toxic. If your child is wondering whether their friendship with someone is toxic, highlight the warning signs that a relationship has gone belly up.

> Michael's definition of a bad friend is someone who:
> - has an irritated manner towards life
> - chatters about others or about your child in a negative way
> - critiques your child, either subtly or overtly
> - constantly reminds your child of their past failures
> - tries to manipulate your child into feeling a certain way or doing things they don't want to do
> - stresses everyone around them
> - requests too much, without giving anything back.

Above all, parents need to give their Year 7 permission to run a mile if they have a friend or peer who is clearly into things that they know are just wrong. If such a person is a close friend, of course this can be difficult. But your child should not nurture a friendship with someone they know is making a deliberate choice to do things that are dangerous or unhealthy.

If you are concerned about an unhealthy friendship choice your child has made

Raising this issue can be like stepping over broken glass! Why? Because if you kick up a fuss about your distaste for your child's friend, they are more than likely going to up the ante on that friendship and spend more time with this friend just to spite you. If you are genuinely concerned about your child's choice, find an appropriate time to speak to them gently about their friendships in general.

If you have concerns about a specific person, ask your child what qualities they like about that person (without casting your own judgements). Simply asking the question, 'Is this who you want to be like?' can offer your child the opportunity to consider the benefits of associating with this person.

Banning your child from being friends with someone is not usually the answer. Instead, encourage them to seek out a range of friends. Often, your child will naturally work things out for themselves when it comes to making good friendship choices. What may seem appealing about a negative person in the early stages will hopefully wear off.

Peer pressure

We have stressed that obtaining, retaining and maintaining good relationships is a key component of your Year 7's psychological wellbeing, but occasionally trying to be part of a new social group can turn sour.

Peer pressure occurs when your Year 7 is doing something they wouldn't normally do, or are not doing something they'd like to do, simply so that they will be accepted by the people they hang out with. Suspending their values, attitudes and beliefs, relenting in the face of pressure from these new 'friends', in the hope that they will be accepted into this group can leave them feeling remorseful, ashamed, mortified, disconcerted or even scared.

Think back to their first days in preschool or when they were just starting out in primary school. Someone says, 'Throw that sand on Johnny!' Your child looks down and sees that they are in a sandpit. Just near them are two things: first, there's a lot of sand, and second, they notice a fellow sandpitter. Must be Johnny! The bully wants them to help him out, to hassle the other kid in the sandpit.

'Yeah, go ahead!' the bully repeats to them. 'Throw sand on that kid next to you. In his face! Cmon!' What did they do?!

Peer pressure began then, back in the sandpit. It was the pressure to do someone's bidding, to throw sand on someone else, to become a slave to another's plans and desires. Interesting, isn't it? You see, peer pressure doesn't just magically appear on day one of Year 7, despite the bad reputation that secondary school years can have.

Back there in the sandpit, your child made the right choice (hopefully!) to hold off on the sand throwing and to make their own decision. So too, in secondary school, they will be better off resisting the temptation to follow the pressure of another, or of a group of others.

As they go through secondary school, the choices they face might be a little more advanced, like whether to follow friends and go out of bounds during recess, for example. Your Year 7 will always have a choice to make when it comes to peer pressure. In secondary school, the pressure might just be another step up: Do they make a decision not to attend a Science class? Do they wag school with a group of mates? Do they leave the school grounds and have a cigarette?

Don't be fooled into thinking that entry to secondary school equals a massive weight of pressure to do things they don't want to do. Your child always has a choice about the decisions they will make.

It's a great idea for parents to discuss these decisions with their children before they will be faced with them. Parents can help their Year 7s by encouraging them firstly to think about what type of person they want to be. Do they want to be a person who is often known as a 'sheep' and just does what people tell them to do? Another question you can ask of your young person is, 'Is that who you want to be known as?'

Parents should also discuss with their young person responses to the question, 'What to do if . . . (or what to do when . . .)?'

For example, what to do 'if' you are asked to wag a day of school? Will they agree? What will they get out of it? What will the consequences be? Discussing this with your secondary schooler and coming up with some possible responses gives them a script, which can help them with their confidence long before they are ever put on the spot.

Sheep don't want to look silly in front of the flock for taking a stand so they just go along with it anyway. Parents can encourage their children not to be like that. Help them decide now that they will always make the best decision, no matter what. That way, it won't be so difficult when they are faced with the pressure to do something they are not comfortable with.

Choose your influences

If we hang around negative people all the time, chances are high that we will soon become fairly negative people ourselves. In fact, other people's attitudes and opinions can have a huge impact on us.

Most of us will be able to remember when we were put in a group to work on a school project. You may have found that you were with two highly unmotivated people. Often, the motivated person is dragged down by the rest of the group's negativity and lack of focus. There is a big difference in a group's productivity as soon as there are two motivated people, even if they are paired with a fairly negative and unmotivated person. The positive people will quite often motivate the team to achieve its collective best.

The lesson here is simple: the people we choose to spend our time with have great influence – both positive and negative – on us. What sort of people will your Year 7 choose to hang out with?

Case study

Jasmine had started hanging with a negative crowd. They were part of a local gang whose members spent a lot of time at the local railway station, harassing others, smoking and using foul language.

Most of the railway teens lived in government-funded housing for troubled youth. The way they saw it, they were free from rules and restrictions, all the time. That's what they told Jasmine, who they welcomed into their group. She believed them. Their life looked pretty sweet. Back at home, her parents had rules and restrictions – she felt that the rules were holding her back.

Jasmine soon began allowing these negative influences to change her attitude throughout her life, affecting the way she spoke to parents and teachers. Her parents noticed that she was behaving in a more defiant way towards them, ignoring requests to complete her homework, and spending time after curfew secretly on social media engaging with these young people. She began to dress differently and care less about her image.

Within a few months, Jasmine began to feel uncomfortable about her changed attitude. She knew deep down that she was causing tension within her family because of her poor attitude, and she could see that she really did have loving and supportive parents who just had her best interests at heart. She soon terminated contact with the railway teens and came back to spending more time with her family and restoring the relationship. For Jasmine, it had been a time of learning some valuable lessons about choosing your influences.

If your Year 7 elects to hang around with the wrong people for too long, they will soon become just like the people that you have warned them against. If they choose to spend their time with a person who does not care about school or achieving good results, soon your child will not care much about them either.

Parents need to encourage their secondary schooler to make a choice, instead, to spend their time with people who have a positive influence on their life and self-image. They should spend time with friends who build them up rather than tear them and others down.

IT'S HARD TO SOAR WITH THE EAGLES WHEN YOU RUN WITH THE TURKEYS...

Q&A time

My son really enjoys reading at lunchtimes as it gives him a break from everything, and he can't seem to put his book down. But he is new in secondary school and really wants to make friends with new people. What should he do?

That's a really great question, and this is actually quite a common problem among many students (those who love reading, anyway).

Encourage him to choose one or two lunchtimes, or recesses, per week in which he can read or hang out in the library. For the others, get him to keep those days free for socialising and making new friends. It's okay to read, and you should encourage that, however, making friends and interacting with other students is just as important because he will be building up a social and support network.

The same could be said if he loved drawing or any other activity that can be done in isolation. It's important for him to have interests that he can do by himself, but make sure he allows plenty of time to be social, too.

My daughter has a really great friend at school, and they usually enjoy hanging out together. But sometimes her friend goes off with other friends at recess and leaves my daughter out completely. How should she handle this? It's making life at school awful!

Social life at school and friendship issues can cause a lot of heartache during secondary school. In fact, it'd be pretty rare if a student didn't experience being left out of a social group at some stage. So what you can emphasise first of all is that she is not alone here!

Sometimes, friends want to expand their social network a bit. That's not to say that they like your daughter any less, but it certainly can feel pretty horrible and isolating at the same time.

Try to get her to branch out on her own a bit too. Encourage her to look for other students who might seem a bit on the outer or don't seem to have many social groups. She could certainly use this as an opportunity to make other new friends. Rather than replacing her existing friends, this will allow her to broaden her social network. She might be surprised by the new friends she will make along the way.

GOSSIP

'Whoever gossips to you
will gossip about you.'
—*Spanish proverb*

Hurtful gossiping can be one of the most difficult parts of being an early adolescent. A definition I use for gossip is anything that you wouldn't be perfectly happy to say in front of the person involved.

Most importantly, our young people need to know that sometimes the effect of gossip is much longer-lasting than the time it takes for the comment to be made. A few years ago I was watching an American talk show. The guest on the program that day was

a woman in her early forties who had been bullied quite badly by a girl who spread hurtful gossip about her during their senior years at school. The gossip was indeed so hurtful and damaging that it kept this woman stuck in a rut. It was like a tape playing the same messages over and over in her mind. The negative messages told her she had no worth and was a failure, a horrible example of a girl, and that her mistakes in secondary school would forever define her. She was not able to progress in her life, hold down successful employment or stable relationships. The show's host actually tracked down the girl responsible for spreading the hurtful rumours all those years earlier and finally the victim had an opportunity to confront her tormentor face-to-face. Incredulous, the woman who had bullied her had no recollection whatsoever of the victim, or the lies that she had spread.

Being gossiped about can be one of the most soul-destroying things a person can experience. It can be a bit like lighting a match in the middle of a forest. At first, only a few small twigs are lit and a small flame grows, then that flame catches onto another branch and before you know it, the whole forest is on fire. This has of course become a much wider-reaching and more sinister possibility with the introduction of social media, which casts a much broader net of social interaction. Social media can spread gossip and rumours within minutes to any online connections. It can also have devastating results, as young people can feel completely ruined by such hurtful lies.

Many secondary schoolers, with their lack of emotional maturity and life experience, can feel that being trapped in a web of gossip is an inescapable situation and this can sadly lead to instances of self-harm and even loss of life.

Do you remember the game Broken Telephone, in which a group of children sit in a circle and a message is passed from one person to the next? As the message is quietly passed along, bits and pieces of the original message get left out or changed. By the time the message makes its way around the circle back to the first speaker it may not sound anything like the original sentence.

Gossiping is a lot like that game. As people pass on information about another person, they can often add their own slant on the story or exaggerate parts to make themselves sound better. By the time the hurtful gossip gets around, it can be very far removed from the actual truth and that's where extreme damage can be done to the person being talked about.

There is a really simple guideline for working out if something is gossiping or not. Encourage your teenager to ask themselves the following questions before continuing to pass on information:

'Will this information build the other person up (make them feel great about themselves), or damage their self-image? Will it make that person feel good or bad?'

It's pretty simple, really. They will know, in their gut, whether the information is helpful or not. Ask them to use their intuition.

Unfortunately social media can be a quick and disastrous medium for spreading gossip and hurtful rumours at lightning speed. This is where it is important for parents to monitor what their child is doing online and ensure that they are not tucked away in their bedroom for hours, where they may have the opportunity to read and perhaps engage in unhelpful conversations. Make sure to be their 'friend', and have an agreement on what is okay to post and what is not.

As parents, at this stage of your child's life, you have a crucial role in helping them navigate the murky waters of gossip.

Teach your child not to be a gossip

Teaching your child to not gossip about others will not simply be a one-off conversation. In many cases, your child may not realise they are gossiping and may believe they are merely relaying information they have heard from others. If you hear your child gossiping about a friend or peer at school, simply ask them these questions: 'In what ways are you building this person up right now with your words? If they were sitting in this room right now, would you still be having the same conversation?'

Your child may scoff at this, but you can explain to them that the sentiment is still the same. If you think repeating this information can help the other person, or build them up in some way, go ahead. If not, stop it.

Avoid gossiping yourself

Your child is going to be much more influenced by what they see *you* do and how you behave than by any conversations you may have with them about this topic. If you yourself are constantly discussing the lives of others and making judgements about them in front of your offspring, do not be shocked if they follow in your footsteps. Your own words and behaviour towards your peers are being watched and often emulated.

Deal with gossip

If your secondary schooler is the topic of hurtful gossip or rumours this can hit them quite hard. It can be tough to turn up to school, or any environment for that matter, when you are well aware that peers are discussing your personal business. If you find your child is distressed or experiencing a change in mood due to gossiping, it's important to have a conversation with them about what is occurring. Why do people gossip? Because they are trying to build themselves up at the expense of others, by painting others in a less than glowing light. Help your child understand that they are not to blame. When the gossip relates to a person at your child's school, a quick email to your child's pastoral care teacher or year level coordinator will keep them in the loop about this behaviour. It's important to not be accusatory in your communication with the school. However, it is important that they are made aware of any gossip, as information such as this can often form part of a puzzle and be indicative of a pattern of behaviour by a student or students.

BULLYING

Bullying is an ongoing misuse of power in relationships. It can be enacted through repeated verbal, physical and/or social behaviour that causes physical and/or psychological harm. Bullying can come from a single individual or it can be a group misusing their power over one or more persons.

Bullying can happen in person or online, and it can be obvious (overt) or hidden (covert). Bullying in any form or for any reason can have long-term effects on those involved, including bystanders. (It is worth noting that single incidents and conflicts or fights between equals, whether in person or online, are not defined as bullying.)

Bullying is, unfortunately, something that many young people associate with secondary school. A 2018 report by ARACY found that 15.3 per cent of those aged 15–19 were very or extremely concerned about bullying. And that's a big shame because many students make it through secondary school without any experience of bullying whatsoever. When it does happen, it can occur in primary school just as easily as secondary, or even in the workforce. The Alannah and Madeline Foundation found that 27 per cent of young people report they are bullied every two weeks or more often. It is not just face to face harassment, many young people who bully offline also bully online. What is more, some young people who are bullied sometimes go on to engage in bullying others. Bullying can seriously damage physical, social

DEALING WITH BULLIES 101:

'SAY, HAVE YOU GUYS SEEN
THESE YOUTUBE KITTENS?
... SO CUTE!'

and emotional health in the short term, and also have serious long-term consequences. Young people who bully are, over time, much more likely to engage in ongoing anti-social behaviour and criminality, have issues with substance abuse, demonstrate low academic achievement and be involved in future child and spouse abuse, as found by Suzanne Vassallo using research from the 2012 Australian Temperament Project.

Bullying is often associated with secondary school, where it can seem more prevalent because there are usually more students and a greater number of social groups that can lead to more problems. When most of us think of bullying, it's easy to think of someone being backed into a corner of a classroom when the teacher is out of the room, an image of someone being verbally threatened or physically assaulted.

I remember, as a Year 7 student, new to my secondary school, being locked in the storeroom cupboard of the classroom by a tall student. It wasn't a life defining, traumatic moment. It was simply a case of one student using their perceived 'power' over another student. This is exactly what a bully does. They are really just playing out their own fears of not being enough and trying to make another person feel inferior or insignificant – hence locking a new student in a cupboard for a few minutes as an example of a power play.

But while physical, overt bullying does still unfortunately occur, the covert, emotional type of bullying can be just as hurtful and can leave lasting memories and effects.

Parents of students in Year 7 need to use the power of the narrative (storytelling) to remind their children of the potential impact of such behaviour on others. Almost all countries have examples of young people who were subject to on- and offline harassment to such an extent that they chose to end their lives. While I am not claiming that these young people were 'bullied to death', bullying can certainly play a role as a catalyst for individuals who may have pre-existing issues. In 2013, it was a 14-year-old girl, Hannah Smith, who captured the attention of the UK media. In the US it was a 13-year-old girl, Megan Meier, and in Canada it was 15-year-old Amanda Todd. The most recent Australian example was Amy Jayne 'Dolly' Everett who, on 3 January 2018, died by suicide, allegedly after vicious bullying at the hands of her peers. In the days leading up to her funeral, her father, Tick, wrote a Facebook post imploring that those students who believed that bullying was not serious should 'come to our service [for Dolly] and witness the complete devastation you have created'.

When bullying does occur – on- or offline – there is often a group of other students who are witness to what transpires, sometimes referred to as the bystanders. How these students respond can determine whether the behaviour stops or continues. Research suggests that schools can play a key role in increasing the likelihood that bystanders will respond constructively – but it all starts with parents.

Parents should discuss the importance of being the type of person that doesn't stand by and watch this kind of behaviour occur. If your Year 7 witnesses bullying, online or offline, they are a bystander. Parents should tell their offspring that even one person's support can make a big difference for someone who is being bullied. When people who are bullied are defended and supported by their peers, they are less anxious and depressed than they would have been otherwise.

Examples of bullying

- Verbal or written abuse (such as targeted name-calling or jokes, or displaying offensive material)
- Violence (including threats of violence)
- Sexual harassment (unwelcome or unreciprocated conduct of a sexual nature, which could reasonably be expected to cause offence, humiliation or intimidation)
- Homophobia (or other hostile behaviour towards students relating to gender and sexuality)
- Discrimination, including racial discrimination (treating people differently because of their identity)
- Cyber bullying (any of the above, either online or via mobile phone)

What is not bullying?

- Mutual conflict that involves a disagreement, but not an imbalance of power (unresolved mutual conflict can develop into bullying if one of the parties targets the other repeatedly in retaliation)
- Single-episode acts of nastiness or physical aggression, or aggression directed towards many different people
- Social rejection or dislike – it is not bullying unless it involves deliberate and repeated attempts to cause distress, exclude, or create dislike in others

Things you can do if your secondary schooler is being bullied

Listen to their story

Try to listen to the whole story without interjecting. Be empathetic and composed, and affirm what your Year 7 says. Ask them what they would like to have happen before you start making suggestions.

Have a discussion about what transpired

Talk to your Year 7 about the situation but do not let your feelings get involved, as this might discourage your child from talking to you. You'll help them more if you stay cool. Remind them it's normal to feel upset. The key parental support message is that it's never okay to be bullied, and it's *not* their fault.

Document what happened

Write down or record all occurrences of bullying, including what happened, as well as when and where, who was involved and if anybody saw what happened.

Collaborate with the school to find a resolution

You need to ascertain if the school is aware of the bullying and if they have implemented anything to resolve the situation. Go the school's website and check out their bullying policy. Secure an appointment with your child's teacher, year level coordinator or school wellbeing person. Make a follow-up appointment to ensure that they take action. Remember, they are there to help. Even if your child doesn't want you to do anything, you should still follow up with the school: you are the adult and your child has a right to learn in a safe environment.

Find other ways to support your child

Instruct your Year 7 to use neutral language or, if appropriate, joking language in response. Practise 'fogging', where if someone says something horrible, your child simply replies with, 'Maybe' or, 'If you say so' and then walks away. Also clarify that more often than not it is better to stay away from dangerous situations if possible. Never offer to confront the bully yourself.

Inspire your Year 7 to get involved in extra-curricular activities such as art, music, dance, drama, sports or hobbies where they can spend time with other young people. Having one set of friends in school and another outside is a great thing for anyone in Year 7.

What the students have to say . . .

I was bullied during years 6–8 at school. I hid it from my parents for 3–5 months, and then it got serious. It was only verbal, but it still hurt. I am a sensitive person, and I try not to take everything personally but it is hard sometimes. My bullying experience was kind of like a rollercoaster, it went up and then it calmed down for a day before it went crazy again. There were two girls in particular who would exclude me when I thought I was their friend, they would throw food in my hair, but I just laughed with them. They would draw devil horns on my head when I was in the school newsletter. I started to get really sick of it and physically tired by it, so I told my mum. At the time I didn't think it was bullying, and when my mum said it was bullying I denied it. I started to self-harm without anyone knowing. After eight months of being bullied on and off, I wanted revenge. One day the class was outside and I said something mean and personal to one of the girls. I got badly punished for it because the teachers didn't fully understand. My advice is stand up for yourself and tell an adult who can help you out, and please don't self-harm. I am good now but it is not okay for you to hurt yourself, even in the darkest days.

Jane

When your child is the bully

It's hard for any parent to believe that their child is the one engaging in bullying behaviour towards other young people, but sometimes it happens. On finding this out you might feel angry, frustrated, hurt, shocked, worried, fearful or defensive – these are all normal reactions. However, it is how you respond that is pivotal.

What to do

- Try to stay relaxed. Remember, the behaviour is the problem, rather than your Year 7.
- Take time for yourself to process how it makes you feel, so that when you talk with your child, you are calm. Try talking it over first with a trusted friend or going for a walk.
- Manage your reactions and get the facts by talking with your child and working to resolve the situation.
- Make sure your Year 7 understands that bullying behaviour is wrong, and why.

- Try to recognise the reasons why your Year 7 has behaved in this way and find strategies to address problems.
- Support your child to look at it from the other's perspective, for example, 'How would you feel if . . .'
- Help your child think of substitute behaviours.
- Provide proper boundaries for their behaviour; set rules at home around disrespect, violence and aggression.
- Assist your Year 7 to articulate precisely what they did and to be answerable and responsible by apologising and finding a way forward.
- Make well-defined, modest, precise rules. Offer reinforcement when rules are obeyed, such as verbal praise.
- Define age-appropriate consequences, such as no Xbox, phones, tablets, or some other negative sanction. Be prepared to enforce them.
- Give your Year 7 some goals and reward positive behaviour. For example, 'If you behave then you will be allowed more pocket money, or a treat of some kind.'
- Monitor and supervise. Keep an eye on your Year 7's actions, whereabouts and friends, including their internet and mobile phone use (these are fast becoming one of the key tools in bullying behaviour). Talk to the school about options for extra playground or class supervision.

STAYING HEALTHY

'If you've had a tough day, grab an early night. It can do
wonders for your mind and body.'
—*Sharon Witt*

Imagine you have finally purchased your dream car, a thing of
beauty. You drive it around with pride and visit all your friends. You
cannot, however, be bothered washing it, so a mountain of dirt and
grease builds up over the first year. You drive and drive the car, but
you forget to check the oil and water, not to mention filling the tank
with petrol.

How far do you think you would get? I can tell you now that
it would not be long before your prized car would stop. It cannot
continue to run without constant attention and good fuel.

A Year 7 body is a bit like a car. Year 7s need constant fuel and
care in order to keep them running at their optimum. We read once
how we should look after our bodies because they are the only
houses we have. We only get one body, so we really need to encourage our Year 7s to take the time to care for it.

Most parents realise the importance of keeping their early adolescent clean and healthy, especially during their secondary school
years as they grow into a young adult. As your child enters puberty,
you'll notice an increase in their capacity to sweat – particularly
from their underarms. It is now important for them to bathe regularly. For girls, as they begin menstruation, it is even more important
for them to shower daily. They should not neglect their teeth, either!
Teeth are an important part of our health and need to be brushed

and flossed daily to remove plaque and prevent bad breath.

If your teenager finds that they sweat a lot, get them to use a good antiperspirant deodorant under their arms. You should also remind them to clean their face daily to remove the grime and dirt that builds up in their pores.

Tips for staying healthy

- Get plenty of sleep (aim for 8–10 hours).
- Shower daily.
- Use a good antiperspirant deodorant.
- Wash and clean your face daily.
- Brush and floss your teeth twice daily.
- Drink plenty of water (aim for eight glasses per day).
- Eat well during the day and avoid too many sugary treats.

On the issue of body shape and size, it's a good idea to not get caught in that mental battle. Parents need to set a good example: it is hard not to buy into body shaming, and social media and the internet have made it ten times more difficult to escape. Being conscious of negative body talk around your Year 7, not making negative statements about your own body or other people's, as well as modelling a healthy acceptance of your own body shape can make all the difference.

Of course, if your secondary schooler is worried about a friend's health, make sure they know to tell an adult. Otherwise, we need to convince our young person to try to ignore any negative behaviour around people's bodies as it will only seek to bring them down, and they don't need that.

Get a good night's sleep

A common trap for some Year 7s is staying up to all hours listening to music, watching YouTube clips, gaming, or chatting to friends via online apps. But your early adolescent needs to realise that sleep is food for the brain.

Keeping track of sleep quality and quantity is not just for babies. The National Sleep Foundation suggests that teenagers need 8–9 hours sleep a night but, in reality, what they often get is closer to 5–7 hours. They found that 59 per cent of Year 7s were getting less than the recommended 8–9 hours of sleep on school nights. According to Professor Russell Foster, sleep expert and co-author of *Sleep: A Very Short Introduction*, 36 per cent of your Year 7's entire life will be spent asleep.

Sleep is the single most important experience that can affect your child's behaviour. A sleep deficit can impact a young person's attention and memory capacity, increase aggressive or withdrawn behaviours, and increase their risk of being overweight or obese. Even more seriously, sleep loss has been linked to an increased risk of depression, anxiety and drug abuse. Hectic schedules don't help, with some Year 7s juggling after-school activities, sport, jobs, homework, and early school start times. But there is also a physi-ological basis for the lack of sleep at this time: delayed release of melatonin (the 'sleep-inducing' hormone), which starts occurring from puberty onwards, means that teenagers don't feel sleepy until later in the evenings. Therefore they delay bedtimes, with the result being that, according to Professor Foster, as many as four-fifths of teenagers report being sleepy upon waking, impacting on their ability to function optimally at school.

The consensus among psychologists is that sleep is without a doubt the single most important study skill going around. If your Year 7 is sleep-deprived after they have tried to learn a task, their ability to learn that task is enormously diminished. Sleep is very important for memory consolidation.

However, sleep does much more than just help to consolidate and retrieve memories. Research cited by Professor Foster has found that people's ability to come up with novel solutions to complex problems is hugely heightened by a good night's sleep. Sleeping at night also enriches their creativity, as neural and synaptic connections are linked and strengthened and those that are less important tend to fade away.

Sleep tips

- Help your Year 7 create optimal conditions for sleep in their bedroom. Make sure the room is cool, dark and quiet.
- Enforce a technology ban in the bedroom. Backlit screens can interfere with melatonin production, so all devices need to be switched off one hour before bed and left to charge in a public room. Keep computers and TVs out of the bedroom and avoid taking internet-enabled devices to bed.

- Encourage some wind-down time before sleep. Tackling that really hard Maths problem then falling into bed is going to be less sleep-friendly than a quiet period of reading or listening to music. Adolescents can train their minds for sleep by establishing triggers such as:
  - having a warm bath
  - reading
  - drinking warm milk or Milo
  - listening to calming music (not heavy metal!)
  - using an appropriate sleep app
- Set a regular sleep routine and try to stick to it. Encourage your Year 7 to keep regular sleep and wake times, and to fall asleep in bed (rather than on the couch).
- Be aware that sleep problems can be a sign of mental health problems. For example, Year 7s with depression often have difficulty falling asleep and getting up in the morning. Consult your GP if you are worried.
- Don't offer caffeinated drinks, including energy drinks, cola or coffee within six hours of bedtime. Avoid late night eating. Experts such as Professor Foster suggest no caffeine drinks after midday.

Trying to last through the rigours of daily school life is a lot more difficult when you are not feeling energised. So do your Year 7 a favour and give yourself permission to be very tough on the issue of sleep – it really should be non-negotiable.

Diet

Be mindful of your child's diet. Researchers have found that there is a link between mood and food. Mood-boosting foods include fruit, probiotics, vegetables, legumes, wholegrain cereals, nuts and seeds, and foods with polyunsaturated fatty acids and omega-3 (found in fish), as recommended by the Australian Dietary Guidelines.

Whole (unprocessed) diets higher in plant foods, healthy forms of protein and fats are consistently associated with better mental health outcomes because these foods are the foundation of health, and contain the many thousands of nutrients needed for the optimal functioning of the body and brain. These diets are also high in fibre, which is essential for gut microbiota. We're increasingly understanding that the gut is really the driver of health, including mental health, as shown in research from 2018 by D Lin et al., so keeping fibre intake high through the consumption of plant foods is very important.

According to the Australian Bureau of Statistics in 2018, only 2.5 per cent of children aged 5–14 and 3.3 per cent of people aged 15–24 eat enough fruit and vegetables. At the risk of being called the food police, I would plead with parents to be wary of the sugar content of what their secondary schooler consumes. A study by Public Health England in 2019 found that the average 10-year-old has consumed as much sugar as the recommended limit for an 18-year-old – the equivalent of eight excess sugar cubes a day. When it comes to adolescent diets, an Australian Psychological Society study from 2016 found that only 19 per cent of teenagers ate sufficient fruit and vegetables and one in five adolescents (19 per cent) consumed soft drinks almost every day or more.

In these days of junk and processed foods, make sure your young person eats at least three serves of fruit and vegetables per day. Get them involved with cooking, have them pick out some fruits and vegetables they like at the shops and keep fewer treats in the cupboard.

Our bodies are made up of more than 50 per cent water. This means that we need to ensure we replace our fluids constantly. Drinking two litres (eight glasses) of water per day is recommended.

Try suggesting to your secondary schooler that they fill a 1.5 litre plastic bottle with water at the beginning of the day. Encourage them to carry this bottle around with them and drink from it wherever they go. If this sounds too much, they can fill a smaller bottle regularly throughout the day. If water is too boring for them, cut a small slice of lemon or lime and pop it in the bottle. Many teachers in secondary school will encourage their students to keep up their water intake during the day (some will even allow a water bottle on the desk in class), especially during the warmer months.

Exercise

Remind your Year 7 to keep their body healthy by making sure they exercise regularly. In an age where so many young people are spending extremely large amounts of time engaged online, ensure your young person gets outside and actually *moves*. The 2016 Report Card on Physical Activity for Children and Youth by Schranz et al. reported that Australian children are among the least active in the world, ranking 21st out of 38 countries, with fewer than 1 in 5 children aged 5–17 meeting the recommended sixty minutes of physical activity each day. Fewer than one in four Year 6 students have mastered physical milestones such as catching, throwing, sprinting, jumping and side galloping.

Our 'screenagers' fare even worse: a VicHealth report from 2018 showed that 92 per cent of teenagers are not meeting their recommended amount of daily physical activity and may be the first generation with a shorter life expectancy than their parents. Obesity continues to increase, with 31.6 per cent of those aged 5–24 being obese in 2015, up from 29.6 per cent in 2007.

Given that 2018 research shows that more than two in three Australian children and teenagers are driven to school, it is a good idea to encourage your Year 7 to walk or cycle to school if possible, and to other places as often as they can, and try to get them involved in a regular sport. (An online game does not count!) Interestingly, a survey by LiveLighter found that more than half of parents thought it was important that children be able to walk to school without an adult, but less than one third thought it was safe for them to do so.

Some ideas for getting active:

- Walk your dog, or somebody else's.
- Go for a run.
- Go for a bushwalk with friends.
- Take an aerobics class.
- Take up a sport. e.g. netball, baseball, football, soccer, dancing, gymnastics, boxing, wrestling.
- Join the local gym.
- Try rowing or canoeing.

Stress

There is no doubt that entering secondary school can be a very stressful time. As we have pointed out, Year 7s are coping with huge changes, including:

- Secondary school pressure (this can include a fear of failure, concern about the tougher academics and increasing work load, social pressures, uncertainty about the future, and worries about getting into university)
- Homework pressures
- New school environment
- New teachers
- Physical changes (puberty)
- Emotions
- Parents
- Friendships

It is really important that they find healthy outlets for dealing with any stress that they feel. Some Year 7s deal with stress by exercising or talking with friends. Make sure your Year 7 finds the outlet that best suits them, and make sure they take action. One of the biggest stress indicators is illness, so make sure they take stress seriously and keep a check on their health.

What the students have to say . . .

Coming from a girl who stresses over the smallest things, Year 7 is definitely very stressful. There are new teachers, new classrooms, new students, more homework and, all in all, more stress. You are always worried about getting homework done in time. And you are worried that if you don't hand it in on time, you would get a detention – just like that.

Faith

Signs of stress:

- Inability to sleep properly
- Not being able to eat – disinterest in food
- Lack of interest in friends and things that you usually enjoy doing
- Crying often or feeling down in the dumps
- A feeling of being unable to cope

If your child is experiencing any of the aforementioned symptoms for a few weeks, they could be struggling with stress. It is important that they talk with their teacher or school counsellor. It would also be good for them to visit their local doctor to get a thorough physical examination. (If stress becomes a real problem refer to page 195 about dealing with anxiety.)

Stress busters

If your child is feeling a bit stressed, try some of the following solutions:

- Exercise is great for relieving stress, because their body will release its own natural 'feel-good' chemicals. It also helps the blood flow better throughout their body, giving it a great boost.

- Have a couple of early nights: if they are stressed, this could be a sign that their body needs a bit of a rest. Make them a warm drink, grab a good book and encourage them to read for a little while before having a good, long sleep. They need between eight and ten hours sleep per night to feel well rested and stress-free. Make sleep a priority, and their other priorities will fall into place.
- Eat well: fill their body with lots of fruit and vegetables. This may sound a bit boring, however, spending a few days giving your body extra minerals and vitamins will help restore it.
- Download their favourite comedy movie for them: laughter also releases your body's natural endorphins, which will help make them feel better.
- Do something they love doing: What is their passion? They could paint, draw, write, hike, ride, or make something.
- Spend a day out with friends: get them to go shopping, skateboard, ride their bike, go bushwalking; just hanging out together with mates can be therapeutic.

The best apps we've found for managing and reducing stress:

- Smiling Mind
  (https://www.smilingmind.com.au)
  Smiling Mind is a free mindfulness meditation app developed by psychologists and educators to help bring balance to your life; it's very youth friendly.

- Breathe2Relax

  Breathe2Relax is a smartphone app with instructions and exercises in diaphragmatic breathing, a documented stress-management skill. Includes detailed information on the effects of stress on the body.

- Sanvello

  (https://www.sanvello.com)

  Sanvello provides guided deep breathing and muscle relaxation exercises, daily anti-anxiety activities, and tools including a mood tracker. Year 7s can record their own thoughts, which can help them understand their thinking patterns and recognise possible anxiety triggers.

THE POWER OF SETTING GOALS

'We grow in many ways by setting goals and working on them consistently.'

—*Sharon Witt*

As your child enters secondary school they are provided with the perfect opportunity to learn the valuable art of goal setting. This is a lifelong skill that, when practised repeatedly and mastered, will see them achieve the tasks before them and be best situated to have a successful secondary school experience.

Why should your Year 7 develop the skill of goal setting?

Imagine this: your secondary schooler heads off on a school camp for a week at the beach. It's a hiking camp and they are really excited because they will be hiking with their friends and teacher for three solid days. They arrive at base camp, begin organising their backpacks, then set off with their group for the three-day trek. They begin walking through the glorious bush, and admire the beautiful landscape. After about five hours, however, they begin to wonder how far they have got to go before they arrive at their destination for the day to set up for camp.

They call out to the teacher, 'When will we get to where we're going?'

'I don't know,' the teacher replies, unconcerned. 'I didn't bring a map. I just thought we'd keep walking until we stopped.'

Right about now, you can bet they'll be feeling slightly anxious about where they are all headed. They're clearly lost! And there's probably no mobile phone coverage or battery life left in anyone's phones.

Life can be like a long hike. We can walk for what seems like an eternity and not really get anywhere. That is exactly why setting goals in life is of major importance. We all need to have a clear map that we can follow and revise along the way as we learn more. Choosing something we want in life and making it an actual goal is a really great way to make it happen. That's because we are making a decision to act in order to get what we want. Goals give us direction, keep us focused and motivated, and increase our chances of achieving things.

Why people don't set goals

There are some simple but powerful reasons why some people will not set goals:

- They don't understand the importance.
- They have never set aside the time.
- They don't know how. (Some people think that by just thinking about getting better results in English, it will automatically happen!)
- They are afraid of failing or being rejected by their friends or peers.

What kinds of goals?

Setting goals in Year 7 is basically like setting a road map for where your child wants to go. It helps to give them clear directions so that they can check in with themselves and make sure they are on track. Put even more simply, a goal is a dream with a date attached to it.

For example, your secondary schooler may decide that when they leave school they want to work as a nurse and eventually become a midwife, and help to deliver babies.

Just say they are 14 years old now. They probably already have a bit more of an interest in science than their friends. They can set themselves goals for the next several years along the following lines:

1. Get good results in Science.
2. Study Biology and Science in senior school years.
3. Talk to the careers counsellor at school about all the possible courses that are available to study nursing.
4. Participate in work experience and volunteer work at a local hospital.
5. Work hard to get the results they need to get into the nursing course that they desire.
6. Begin nursing course.
7. Complete nursing degree.
8. Begin training in midwifery.

Goal setting is one of the most important practices students can learn. Your secondary schooler will need to be a goal setter if they want to achieve great things with their life. Otherwise, they risk drifting through school.

Their goal right now might be to become more organised, to work on homework for forty-five minutes each night, to keep their bedroom tidy or to be a good friend to others. Whatever their goals are right now, help them make a commitment to turn them into reality, one step at a time. They do not have to see the entire journey. Just help them take the first step in the direction they want to head. In other words, 'the journey of a thousand miles begins with one step'.

Write down goals

Your Year 7 will give their goals wings when they write them down. That is because they are making a commitment to what they want to work at and achieve next.

For example, maybe their goal is to pass all their end-of-year exams. Their goal sheet might look like this:

1. Find a study partner for English (hardest subject) and Science (second most difficult).
2. Offer to help someone else in Maths (my best subject).
3. Ask my English and Science teachers for some practice exams so I can use these in my study time.
4. Set aside Monday and Wednesday evenings for 1½ hours to revise content.
5. Pass my exams!

They can do this for any of their goals. The point is, they must write them down and commit to seeing them through. All successful people set clear goals. It is not rocket science. It is simply the way to get things done and to achieve results.

It is also important to note that they should attach a date to each goal that they record. Encourage them to write the dates in their diary if that helps. Attaching a date to their goals gives them a clear timeline for completing them. And make sure they write out something new when they have achieved their goal.

Establish rewards for achieving goals

'Laziness may appear attractive, but work gives satisfaction.'
—*Anne Frank*

There are times when working towards the goals they have set for themselves is just plain hard work for early adolescents. No one expects them to work and work and not get anything for it. It is true that they will experience great personal satisfaction from achieving their goals. It is also important, however, to give themselves the occasional reward. Here are a few examples of rewards they could give themselves for achieving goals along the way to their success:

- Treat themselves to a movie or a night out at a sporting event
- Give themselves one or two nights off completing work
- Plan a holiday for when they achieve a major goal
- Get tickets to see a favourite band close to when they expect to achieve a set goal
- Plan a fun night in with a group of friends
- Plan a shopping spree to buy new clothes when they achieve their goal
- Cook one of their favourite foods
- Schedule a night to binge on TV

If their goal is a fairly big one, don't allow them to get put off. Large goals are achieved by breaking them up into smaller, bite-sized, achievable pieces. It can be far too scary to tackle a goal that seems too big from the start. Begin by taking the first small step. Then, once that goal is achieved, take another step. Just keep going. They will get there in the end. Remember, you are also an important role model for your children. Make sure they see you regularly setting your own goals and seeing them through to completion (does that deck out the back finally need to be finished?).

Revisit goals often

'A goal without a plan is just a wish.'
—*Antoine de Saint-Exupéry*

It is no use buying a new outfit and leaving it buried in the back of your wardrobe.

As silly as that sounds, this cobweb-attracting behaviour is a trap your Year 7 should avoid. They must check in with themselves often when it comes to setting goals. It does not work to simply get all enthusiastic, write out their goals and then bury the piece of paper somewhere in their bedroom for the next six months. (If their bedroom is in the same state as most teenagers, they may not find those goals again until the day they move out of home!)

One interesting policy that some schools are introducing is that if a Year 7 forgets something and their parent brings it to school, the school only gives it to them at the end of the day. No rescuing allowed: the onus is on the Year 7 to make sure they have everything organised the night before.

Encourage your teen to put their goals somewhere that is clearly visible, daily. They should not write them on a scrappy piece of paper; instead, encourage them to type them up or make them look important. They may even like to laminate the page, put a magnet on the back and pop it on the fridge door! Better yet, stick it to the back of the toilet door.

Michael's thoughts on a messy bedroom:

While some psychologists interpret untidy rooms as symbolic of the emotional chaos unleashed by the struggle with separation from the parent, most Year 7s are on a long march towards autonomous adulthood, and mastering the clean room is, for many, a tiny insignificant blip on their teenage radar. They are so engrossed during Year 7 with whether they are normal, who they are and where they are going, that they can lose sight of their environment. Many don't even see their rooms. My advice for parents frustrated by messy bedrooms is to take a picture of their child's room when it is tidy and then get that blown up. If you post it on the outside of their door, every time you walk past, it will look perfect!

The point is that you should choose your battlegrounds in Year 7. Fight over things that relate to the safety of your Year 7: sleep, sex, drugs, alcohol, diet, exercise, curfews, internet safety. Parenting should not be an exercise in martyrdom. No one has ever died of an untidy room. Eventually your child will need to find something and be forced to do a mini clean-up. Being organised is a vital life skill that they can learn over time.

CHARISMATIC ADULTS

'Take the first step in faith. You don't have to see the whole staircase, just take the first step.'
—*Dr Martin Luther King, Jr*

Your secondary schooler needs a particular kind of adult in their life. Michael uses the term 'charismatic adult', while I prefer the idea of a cheerleader for your secondary schooler. Others might use the term 'mentor'. Mentors are a bit like coaches for life. They are people who have usually gone before us and are successful in their chosen fields. In cricket terms, they've got 'runs on the board', experience and maturity that we can benefit from.

One of the great pieces of advice parents can give their secondary schooler is to seek out such mentors. All teenagers going into Year 7 need at least one mentor – someone who will make them feel safe, valued and listened to, from whom they can seek advice, and who will follow their journey to success. They need a personal cheerleader.

When I was a teenager, I had a married couple in my church who were able to mentor me throughout my junior and middle school years. They kept an eye on me and were the two people I was able to turn to for advice and help if and when I was ever experiencing difficulty. That was especially helpful with issues relating to getting along with my parents. For Michael, at university,

MR SMITH

FOR SOME REASON HE WAS EVERYONE'S FAVOURITE TEACHER!

he had quite a few mentors who had a major influence on his life. He had two amazing lecturers in particular who believed in him, encouraged him, and ultimately inspired him to pursue psychology.

For Year 7s, a mentor, charismatic adult or cheerleader could be a teacher from their school, an older student, a youth leader, a church pastor, an uncle, aunt, parent, grandparent, or psychologist. They may not even know their mentor right now. But the good news is, with the great advancements in computer technology, they can learn from 'giants' by reading their advice online. They can read comments, articles, and speeches by and about people who have been successful in life.

If your Year 7 wants to be a successful basketball player, help them seek out information about people who are either currently playing or have had previous success. Many elite sports players have produced an autobiography. It might seem old-school but books can be a terrific resource. They are an amazing source of information and inspiration as to how someone has overcome hurdles and challenges and achieved success in their chosen field. We would be very surprised if each successful person they followed did not have at least one great mentor from whom they also learned.

A really innovative idea is to encourage your Year 7 to write an email to someone they admire and whose success they would like to emulate. (Or try an old-fashioned letter – they work particularly well because they are such a novelty these days!) Your Year 7 will probably be surprised that successful people are also normal, everyday people just like us. They have only achieved success because they were driven and set themselves clearly-defined goals. Many successful people get to be that way because they had great mentors in their lives to guide them. Depending on who they are and how busy they are, some may be more than happy to speak to the whole of Year 7 or recommend some speakers, other ideas and directions.

TAKEAWAYS FROM THIS SECTION

- It's okay to make mistakes
  Remind your child that they can and will make mistakes and that these are proof that they are trying. Remind them consistently that there is no mistake they can make that you can't work through together.

- Friendships take time and effort
  Reassure your child that it may take some time to make new friends in secondary school but that they can practise being friendly in order to allow relationships to develop. Chat to your child about the qualities we seek in good friendships.

- Communicate any issues concerning bullying or gossip with school
  If you find that bullying has become part of your secondary schooler's experience, make contact with their pastoral care teacher or year level coordinator so they stay informed.

- Manage their health
  Ensure your secondary schooler receives a good balance of sleep, healthy eating and exercise each day. Remember, their adolescent years are one of their biggest growth stages.

Part 3

Getting the most out of secondary school

TECHNOLOGICAL DEVICES

We live in an age where our children are known as 'digital natives'. They have grown up having access to technology that many parents could only have dreamed of when we were in secondary school. (The first time I saw a giant Apple computer was in a designated room at university.) While this technology provides us with a portal to information that opens up entire new possibilities in education, it also comes with great distractions and responsibility.

It is up to YOU, the parents, to decide if and when your young person has access to their own technological devices. I feel that each parent needs to make a clear decision and be firm around when they will allow access to such devices.

To quote a line from the movie *Spider-man*, 'With great power comes great responsibility.' There is a sense that once you open this Pandora's box, there will be no turning back. So, think through the potential risks and responsibilities before handing over a laptop to your secondary schooler.

Q&A time

When is the best time for my child to have their own mobile phone?

I am often asked this question by responsible, well-meaning parents when running parent seminars. In my opinion, a child does not require a mobile phone until they enter secondary school, and even then, the longer you can hold off the better. Certainly, if they are in primary school and catch public transport, or if you believe your child needs to be able to call you, giving them a 'dumb phone', which is a phone that only has the capabilities of texting and calling (no camera and no connection to the internet), could be beneficial. Owning a phone that has internet capabilities is best left until your child is old enough to fully understand how to navigate it responsibly, in my opinion, no earlier than when they are a teenager. A smartphone should be seen by children as more of a rite-of-passage than an expectation. The decision should also be based on your assessment of your child's personality, emotional maturity and temperament – remember that the greatest predictor of your Year 7's future behaviour is past behaviour. If you do decide to allow your child the privilege of a mobile phone, it's a good idea to draw up a phone contract together, whereby you have an agreement regarding usage, data use and hours of use.

I highly recommend that the phone is placed in a public charging portal with the rest of the family-owned phones each evening. No phones in bedrooms.

Terms of agreement

I would strongly suggest that you first establish some ground rules with your secondary schooler around the use of their device. This includes strict boundaries around times it may be used, what it is used for, and access to the internet if appropriate.

I highly recommend a discussion between yourselves as parents and your child, even before the device is first accessed. Therefore, you can establish clear and consistent guidelines about what is expected from both parents and child.

The following are the child and parent versions of suggested contracts, created by Susan McLean of CyberSafety Solutions (www.cybersafetysolutions.com.au).

Online Family Safety Agreement (Parent)

The internet and digital technology is a wonderful thing and as a family we will need to work together and support each other to make good decisions about what we do online, where we go and what to do if there is a problem. Working together is the best way to make sure that the whole family is as safe as possible when online. This agreement sets out our very clear rules and expectations for both the adults and the children in our family.

I _____, as the parent, carer or guardian of _____ agree that:

1. I will teach my child good online habits by modelling acceptable behaviour myself when online.
2. I will learn how each device works before giving it to my child to use.

3. I will install or activate parental controls, restrictions and/or filters as are applicable for the age of my child.

4. I will try my best to keep up with all the websites, apps, games etc. that my child may want to use and explain rationally why I may say no to a certain site etc. This is my responsibility as a parent.

5. I will set up accounts on all the sites, games and apps that my child has so that I can ensure that the communication is suitable and so I can be part of their digital world.

6. I will engage with my child online, play games with them just as I would in the real world.

7. I will set clear rules and boundaries about what they can do online, where they can go and for how long. This can be amended for both good and bad online behaviour at any time.

8. I will set specific technology-free times such as before school, during meals or Sunday afternoons, for example. I will also obey this rule.

9. I will know all my children's email addresses and passwords in case of emergency. I will not use them unless absolutely required if I believe my child may be in danger or behaving inappropriately online.

10. I will not be a Facebook stalking parent. I will not post pictures or comments that could embarrass my child, I will not add my children's friends to my account, I will not comment on things I see but will speak privately to my child if required. I will not

be angry with my child for what someone else posts to their account.

11.   I will ensure that all internet-enabled technology is kept out of the bedroom. Phones will be handed to me at _____ pm each night and charged with all other phones. They will be given back at a suitable time the following morning. iPods will not be allowed in bedrooms unless the home WiFi is switched off first.

12.   I will ensure that my child is not using apps or websites that have age restrictions that are older than they are.

13.   I will ensure that my child knows what to do if they have a problem online or see something that they know is wrong. I promise to support them and assist them regardless and they will know that they can come to me if they have any problems about anything.

14.   I will assist my child to keep a copy of and report all inappropriate online behaviour to the site in question, the school, the sport club and/or the police. I will teach my child that misusing technology can be a criminal offence.

15.   I will embrace and enjoy technology just as my child does!

_____ Signed
(Parent/Guardian/Carer)

Used with permission
CyberSafety Solutions
www.cybersafetysolutions.com.au

Online Family Safety Agreement (Child)

I _____ aged _____ years

agree that:

1. I will follow all the rules of this agreement and understand they have been set with my safety in mind.

2. I will not start any new accounts, download any apps, or play any online games without first asking permission from my parents.

3. I will not start any new accounts or download any apps that have an age restriction older than me.

4. I will not talk online to people that I do not know in the real world even if my friends do.

5. I will choose a sensible screen name and email address that does not include reference to my location or my age.

6. I will teach my parents as much as I can about the internet and digital technology as it is a lot of fun. I will help them understand things if they are unsure.

7. I will not share my passwords with anyone other than my parents. This includes my friends and siblings. I understand that my parents will not use them except if they feel I am in danger. I will make sure my parents know what accounts I have and what each user or screen name is and also my email address.

8. I understand that there are crimes online and that I can get into a lot of trouble if I misuse technology.

9. I will use technology with respect and responsibility.

10. I will use my manners and be polite when I am online. I will not swear or use mean words and I will not join in if others

are being nasty. If I see cyberbullying I will log off and tell an adult.

11. I will immediately log off and tell my parents if I see something online that is scary, mean, not nice or something that worries me.

12. I will follow my parents' rules for no technology in bedrooms and at certain 'no technology' times of the day. I will log off when my online time is up or if asked to.

13. I will never agree to meet someone that I have only met online. I know that some people online are not who they say they are. I will tell my parents if someone asks to meet me.

14. I will tell my parents if someone asks me to do something that I know is not right or something that bothers me. I will not use the webcam with people that I do not know in the real world.

15. I will not send pictures of myself with my clothes off or in my underwear. I will immediately tell my parents if I am asked to do this.

16. I will tell my parents if I receive rude or naked pictures of anyone.

17. I will not post things online that I would not say in the real world.

18. I will not share personal information online unless my parents say it is OK. This means I do not share my name, address, mobile and home phone number, school, sport club, teacher's names or screen names.

19. I will not open any emails or click links or pop-ups that are from people that I have not met in the real world.

20. I will try to be a good and responsible digital citizen and as a family we will learn and have fun together online.

_____ Signed

(Child)

Used with permission

CyberSafety Solutions

www.cybersafetysolutions.com.au

- -

Mobile phone use in school

In 2018 most of Australia was truly horrified to see mobile phone footage of a 13-year-old girl allegedly assaulting a fellow student. Visuals of the attack in a stairwell at a school in Bega showed the female victim being hurled into a wall, before being punched and kicked while lying on her side. It resembled a Quentin Tarantino movie.

The video was released by the media in the same week as the Hon. Rob Stokes, Minister of Education in NSW, established an Australian-first inquiry into the pros and cons of mobile phone use in schools, which he asked Michael Carr-Gregg to lead. This was a welcome move as, up until very recently, there was no state or territory education department with a policy position on this issue. Views among educators remain divided and the result was that individual school principals were left to decide what they thought was best. Unsurprisingly, the politicians seem to have put this issue into the too-hard basket!

The result is a dog's breakfast of policies right across Australia. Some schools require students to hand in phones at the beginning of the day and collect them at the end of the day. Others require students to keep them in their locker or bag; other institutions allow students to keep them on their person, but not use them in class. Still others allow use during recess and lunchtime, while others don't. Some schools argue that older students (Year 11 and 12) should be allowed to use phones as they have a greater ability to self-regulate.

The debate has not been confined to Australia. Internationally, France has led the way on legislation, with Education Minister Jean-Michel Blanquer announcing a total ban on student mobile phone use in both primary and secondary schools starting in September 2018. Countries like Albania, Greece and parts of the UK have followed suit. The French Minister captured the prevailing European sentiment when announcing the Bill: he said that mobile phones were a technological advance but that they could not be allowed to monopolise our lives. He observed that you can't find your way in a world of technology if you can't read, write, count, respect others and work in a team.

So, what about in Year 7? To what extent does having mobile phones in a Year 7 classroom reduce much-needed physical activity? To what extent is the presence of mobile phones in a Year 7 classroom responsible for loss of concentration? Are they weapons of mass distraction? Does unfettered access to mobile phones in Year 7 exacerbate cyber bullying, image-based abuse, phone theft? Importantly, do mobile phones hamper the ability of young people to interact socially?

Parents and schools must realise that all of these questions are particularly important in Year 7, a time when many students have the psychological resilience of a house of cards.

The NSW inquiry sought to examine the literature and take into account the views of educators, cyber safety experts and parent groups to establish world's best practice. There was already substantial literature outlining the benefits of teacher-directed learning with mobile devices. A 2017 study by Derounian for the University of Gloucestershire revealed that 45 per cent of students believe that the use of phones in class supported their education. One of the biggest advantages listed was the use of phones for accessing digital textbooks and thus engaging more deeply with the material presented.

Ultimately, school is a microcosm of wider society. Just as smartphone use may be inappropriate during meal times, in a family meeting, or during a job interview, it is also inappropriate in the middle of a classroom. Knowing that certain behaviour is suitable in some settings but not in others is at the heart of how young people can better use mobile phones responsibly as they grow up.

After six months, 14 000 survey responses and 80 written submissions from students, parents, academics and teachers, the task of reviewing the use of smartphones in NSW schools came to an end. The Minister agreed to the introduction of strict new bans on smartphones in primary schools. Many individuals and organisations in the cyber safety arena have been campaigning for such a move, based on school's legal duty of care to protect children from digital harms.

A major driver of the recommendations was the research released by the Office of the eSafety Commissioner in May 2019, which surveyed 3 000 young people and found that 24 per cent of 8–12-year-olds had received unwanted contact from strangers online and 15 per cent had been subjected to cyber bullying. But it was not just the predatory behaviour online and cyber bullying that prompted the review team to opt for the ban, it was also the inappropriate sharing of explicit images between students, and the overwhelming number of teachers who argued that mobile phones in schools were an unnecessary distraction.

The recommendation unsurprisingly has the overwhelming support of the Australian Primary Principals Association, many of whose schools had already introduced some form of prohibition, but who now of course have departmental and ministerial backing. The people of NSW should be pleased it has a Premier and Minister who have shown leadership in the area.

Interestingly, one Finnish education expert, Pasi Sahlberg, said he believed mobile phone-related distraction was a main reason for Australia sliding down in PISA rankings. The Program for International Students Assessment is a worldwide OECD study of 15-year-old students' scholastic performance on Maths, Science and Reading across 70 nations. Pasi, unsurprisingly, came out in support of the primary school ban.

On 26 June, 2019, Victoria became the first state to instigate a blanket ban on the use of mobile phones from first bell to last in all state schools. The Minister for Education, James Merlino, announced the reform at McKinnon Secondary College, which has seen the benefits of its mobile phone ban on student learning and social behaviour. According to Principal Pitsa Binnion, school staff report that students are more focused during class and are communicating more in the school yard – what is not to like? They can still use technology through laptops and tablets using the school's internet filter. Mobile phones have been banned for all students at Victorian state primary and secondary schools from Term 1 2020, to help reduce distraction, tackle cyber bullying and improve learning outcomes for students.

Rolling out a state wide policy will provide consistency and certainty for parents, students and school communities. All Victorian state school students will be expected to switch off their phones and keep them securely in their lockers from first bell to last. Should an emergency arise, parents or guardians can contact their child by calling the school. There are exceptions to the ban for students who use phones to monitor health conditions, or where teachers instruct students to bring their phone into the classroom for a particular activity. At all other times phones must be in lockers.

What do we know about Year 7s that will guide their phone usage?

Most Year 7 brains struggle to focus and concentrate on one thing at a time, so it is self-evident that with access to laptops and tablets in their lessons they do not need phones as well. I believe mobile phones should be banned in classrooms, unless specifically being used in an educational context. Certainly, on the basis of what teachers are telling us there is no doubt that the majority want the phones out, claiming that laptops and tablets will do the job and as an added bonus are filtered through the school's network.

It is important to note that all schools have a legal duty of care to provide students in Year 7 with a safe environment in which to learn. The presence of mobile phones in class and at recess and lunchtime is a foreseeable and preventable source of cyber bullying, inappropriate material and image-based abuse, so schools could be sued for a breach of this duty of care, unless they explicitly prohibit the unauthorised use of mobile phones at these times.

I believe that all Year 7s should be required to sit a digital licence (e.g. https://www.digitallicence.com.au) before being allowed to bring their phones to school. Whether this is mandated by law (as it will be in Queensland and NSW), or is adopted by individual schools as a legal protection, it is clear that there is a need for all Year 7s to show that they have the skills, knowledge and strategies to use their phones in a safe, smart and responsible manner.

Few people believe that mobile phones are inherently evil. I acknowledge a range of useful apps and web-based programs that can enhance the wellbeing of young people in Year 7. But I do believe in keeping Year 7s safe, so keeping phones in lockers and bags during the day makes sense. Students can still contact their parents on the way to and from school if need be.

Social media

Social media has become a part of the very fabric of our lives – indeed, if you have a child over the age of thirteen, you are most likely navigating the various intricacies of social media that permeate teenagers' lives. Legally, children need to be aged thirteen to be able to hold a social media account such as Facebook and Instagram; however, anecdotally we know that many children are accessing social media much earlier. Big social media companies like Facebook have to obey the Children's Online Privacy Protection Act (COPPA) – a law created to protect the privacy of children aged under thirteen. The Act was passed by the U.S. Congress in 1998 and took effect in April 2000. The COPPA Rule applies to operators of commercial websites and online services directed to individuals under the age of thirteen that collect personal information from children, and to operators of general websites with 'actual knowledge' that they are collecting information from individuals under the age of thirteen.

Although our children have been born with this technology they are not necessarily well-versed in cyber citizenship skills. In other words, they are technologically savvy but do not necessarily possess the tools, strategies and maturity to appropriately deal with online issues or appropriate protocols. As parents, we have a responsibility to understand the world our children are regularly a part of (some adolescents are spending up to five hours each day on social media!), know what they are doing online and help guide them through any problems they encounter.

The tabloid media and some social commentators have blamed the increasing use of social media for the 70 per cent rise in rates of depression, anxiety and suicidal behaviour among young people. But research on the subject is conflicting.

An analysis by *The Lancet* based on data from the UK Our Future study suggests the correlation is not so direct and much more complex.

I AM EXERCISING!

NAN SMITH

Russel Viner and his colleagues found that social media is associated with mental health issues, but only under certain circumstances, and that this correlation is related to gender. They found that in girls, frequent social-media use does seem to do harm when it led to either cyber bullying and/or inadequate sleep and exercise. But these factors did not seem to have the same effect on boys.

Parents need to know that, while we are not opposed to social media per se, there needs to be an awareness of the amount of time your Year 7 spends on it and the amount of balance that they have in their life. 2018 research from Booker et al. found that Year 7s who spend more than one hour on social media per day are likely to have worse mental health than those who do not.

Furthermore, 20 per cent of young people wake in the night to check their social media feeds, found Power et al. in 2017, and internet addiction – a catch-all term that relates to the compulsive need to spend time online, to the point where relationships, work and health are negatively impacted – is increasingly discussed. Medical and psychological opinion is divided on whether internet addiction exists as a mental disorder in its own right.

Jean Twenge, a psychology professor at San Diego State University, author of *iGen: Why Today's Super-Connected Kids are Growing up Less Rebellious, More Tolerant, Less Happy–and Completely Unprepared for Adulthood–and What That Means for the Rest of Us*, maintains that being online has dramatically changed the lives of young people, irrespective of where they live and their socio-economic status. She argues that excessive use of the internet and social media makes young people isolated and sad and impacts their physical and mental wellbeing.

Others say that this is just another moral panic – similar to the warnings that emerged around television, the gramophone record, jazz music, comic books, Elvis Presley and computer games. At the time it was widely believed that if young people spent time engaging in any of the aforementioned entertainments it would be catastrophic. While there is still a healthy debate among academics and some mental health professionals, really good longitudinal studies using double blind control trials – the gold standard in research of this nature – are still to emerge. Our advice is to exercise common sense.

Common-sense tips:

- Have regular discussions with your secondary schooler about what they are doing online and who they interact with.
- Monitor your Year 7's social media account on a regular basis.
- We recommend you insist on being a 'friend' on their account as part of them having this privilege.
- Monitor the amount of time your child is using social media.
- Tell them that their password is like a toothbrush: don't share it!
- Have a set time when devices are no longer used at night. (If you need to change the home wifi network password after 8 p.m., do it!)
- Have the conversation with your child, 'What would you do if . . . ?'
- Discuss with your child how you would respond if they experienced bullying on social media (or if they made a poor choice online). Many children are reluctant to tell their

parents because they are scared they will lose their online privileges.

- If your child experiences any bullying online or on social media, encourage them to save any information, block the user and report to you. Take your concerns to the school if the offender attends the same school, or otherwise the police.

Sexting

Sexting involves sending sexually explicit messages or images via email, apps, text messages and the like. If the photos are shared, the immediate fallout is usually among the person's peer group, school and local community. However, once photos are sent, there is no way to get them back; once in cyberspace, they become a permanent part of a person's digital footprint. This means that they can forever be linked to that person. Without a doubt, they will resurface when least expected, such as prior to a job interview. As well as the embarrassment that can result from having these pictures shared, the sharing of such images can also be used to cyber bully and harrass the victim. And if this isn't bad enough, the images can then fall into the hands of those with the predilection to sexually offend against children and young people.

Safety tips for parents

- Talk to your children about the consequences of sexting, including warning them about the danger of sexual predators.
- Remind them that sending, receiving or forwarding sexual images is illegal, and that respectful behaviour is just as important when using mobile phones as it is in person.

- Give children clear rules about what they can and can't do with their mobile phone.
- Become familiar with the technology your child is using, such as Facebook, Tumblr, Twitter, Skype etc., and talk to them about privacy/security settings to help protect themselves from bullying/predators. Remember that most phones have instant access to the internet and social networking sites.
- Encourage your children to talk to you or another adult they trust if they have any problems or concerns around texts they have sent, received or forwarded, and reassure them this won't necessarily mean they will be asked to stop using the technology.

Used with permission
CyberSafety Solutions
www.cybersafetysolutions.com.au

GETTING ORGANISED

In life, we need to have some sort of system to get organised, otherwise we tend to feel a bit out of control and not sure what we should do next.

Imagine walking into a doctor's surgery and having to step over a pile of papers, books, rubbish and clothes just to reach the examination chair. I'm guessing you would think that the doctor was not too serious about being a doctor. You might also be concerned if he's hurrying you along when he does see you, or if she's more focused on golf-putting practice than answering the intercom.

Just like with the golf-mad doctor, you are able to tell a lot by looking at a teenager's bedroom. If it's chaos city, that says something about your child's state of mind. Chances are, your teen is probably feeling a bit hectic and confused with life in general.

Here's the thing: with your help and encouragement, your secondary schooler can begin to organise their life better *today*. They can start by organising their bedroom at home. While being organised for a teenager is not the 'be all and end all', it can help them to feel a sense of control in their immediate surroundings. Suggest setting aside an afternoon (or a whole week, if it's that bad!) for your Year 7 to find a home for all their possessions before school starts. Parents can help by buying inexpensive boxes or plastic containers from a local discount shop, or even cover some old shoeboxes in fun paper. Then get labelling!

Make sure they label the boxes clearly so that they know where to find things when they need them.

Things they can organise into boxes:

- Photographs
- School projects
- Make-up
- DVDs and other discs
- Letters and cards from friends and family
- Keepsakes, journals, special cards

They will feel so much better once they begin to organise themselves.

It's true that some young people do not find this easy. It doesn't come naturally to everyone. And that's okay! But it's no excuse for chaos. It might seem like a big job, but they can always ask for help, especially from family members or friends who are better at organising than they are.

As their parent, you may like to offer to spend half a day working with your child, and modelling how to best organise their items. For school, they can use different coloured markers to label different homework subjects and set assignments. As they go, they can tick off work when it has been completed.

Being organised for secondary school

The subject of organisation causes many a student to crumble into a quivering mess on the floor at its mere mention. Okay, well maybe not a quivering mess, but it certainly causes many adolescents stress and worry, especially those who are totally disorganised.

As humans, we are not naturally born as super organised beings. It is very much a learned trait or habit. The great news is that there is a great deal of help out there to get your Year 7 student organised and on top of everything – whether they are about to begin secondary school or they are halfway through and still trying to sort themselves out.

Those students who usually survive quite well with the schoolwork side of secondary school are mostly those who have developed good, solid organisational habits. Don't worry if this doesn't describe your Year 7! If their bedroom and schoolbag resemble the after-effects of a tornado, help is at hand.

What the students have to say . . .

I was always the unorganised kid in primary school but we had table tubs which made it easier for me to get through each class. In secondary school, we had lockers. The locker bays would always be crowded and people would be messing around while I was trying to find the correct books inside my disgusting locker so I'd always panic every time we had to prepare our books for the next period.

Dylan

It is very important to be organised in high school because when you get homework it will be less stressful and you can keep your notes and research clear. You will feel more confident about your work and it will make it easier to revise and study. Don't worry too much about being super organised, just try not to be too messy. Something that is really important in secondary school is to use a school diary. I missed completing many projects and received quite a few detentions in Year 7 because I didn't write my homework in my diary.

Mia

When it comes to helping your child be an organised person, you as their parent can have a great deal of influence. As I have said, your child will be more influenced by what you do than what you say.

Case study

Jill, the parent of secondary school-aged children, is a list maker by nature. She writes a list before she goes to bed every night because she worries that she'll forget important things in the morning otherwise. However, Jill never talked to her own kids about why she does this – it's just a habit she has had for years. One morning, Jill went to leave for work and found a handwritten note taped to the front door, complete with little boxes to tick off next to each point. It was written by her daughter! She hadn't realised until that moment that her kids had always been observing her organisational traits without her being aware of it.

The basics – what they'll need for secondary school

Before starting secondary school, your Year 7 will most likely be given a stationery and book list by their school that will contain all the items required for each of their subjects. Many schools have associations with the school book suppliers, making the process fairly simple: these days you can place an online order and pick up your books at a later date.

These lists are actually an incredible resource for getting students organised before beginning secondary school. They contain all the items your Year 7 will need to do two things: one, they'll keep their teacher happy ('I'm impressed you've got your spare loose-leaf refill sheets, Skye!'); two, they'll make their life easier and might even impress parents ('Skye, as your mother, I am so impressed you knew where to find that spare binder book we bought you!').

You'd be surprised how many students I've come across in my teaching career who arrive at class without the basic and essential materials. For example, they might turn up to an English class without their pencil cases, pens or even a book to write in. How on earth can you expect to gain anything of significance out of a lesson when you don't even have something to write with?

As a teacher, I like to explain to my Year 7 students at the beginning of their secondary school year that I expect them to be 'active learners'. What I mean by that is that you cannot simply turn up to lessons without the appropriate materials and expect to be drip fed information (or be handed a pen and something to write on because you haven't gotten yourself sorted for class!). Part of the deal in entering secondary school is that you will participate in your lessons. Turning up with the necessary tools and books gives the impression that you are organised and ready to learn.

Students who are not prepared for their lessons can often waste ten or so minutes disrupting other students, and the teacher, trying to borrow a pen and something to write on.

While we're on the topic of being prepared for class, encourage your child to avoid bringing things to school that will distract them from getting the most out of their lessons and completing their work. I'm sure you can imagine the items I mean: electronic/hand-held games, mobile phones (probably banned from school anyway), non-school diaries, silly putty, toys, gadgets, hairbrushes, lip gloss, toy cars, tractors and face masks. (Yes, I've seen them all!)

Having been a secondary teacher for almost three decades I can make this statement with absolute assurity: when it comes to a 'make or break' first year in secondary school, organisation has a great deal to do with success. The more prepared your child is, not just for the beginning of the secondary school year, but also in subsequent weeks and months, the better they will succeed. They will be far less stressed and have a better experience during the school days if they are prepared and have all the books and tools they require. I often observe the wheels falling off by mid-year, as some students have lost their school diary, have dwindled down to their final, half-chewed blue pen, and many of their school books are torn and dog-eared, buried in their locker.

Trust me, it's incredible how a five minute clean-up of a student's locker can suddenly reveal pencil cases that were 'stolen' way back in Term 1, along with a towel from a sports day in the same term, a calculator that never seems to make it to class, and that piece of homework that was somehow 'lost'.

Labelling their gear

This might sound like common sense, and I can even hear your Year 7 mouthing something that sounds a lot like 'Duh!' But I'll say it anyway because it's important: label your stuff!

Your child's name is really special – really – and I wish it was on everything they owned. Because, chances are, they're going to lose something, maybe once or even often. And it's going to sit in a lost property box, alone, if they don't put their name on it.

I'm not saying they have to get a labelling machine or even recruit their entire family into a labelling factory line every January before school starts. (But my advice to parents is to invest in a labelling device. Besides the ease of processing labels, they can be fun.) It can be as easy as making up some labels on a computer at home, printing them off in bulk and sticking them on their gear.

There are even some cool online companies that specialise in producing name labels – for everything from folders to lunch boxes. They even make tiny, thin labels that fit perfectly on pens and pencils. Awesome!

Unfortunately, gear gets lost and stolen at school (by kids less organised than yours, of course), so do yourself a favour and set your secondary schooler up for success in this area. It doesn't have to take a heap of effort. Get them to put all their stationery items on a large table or clear a space on the floor, and name each and every piece of stationery. Even the eraser; just use a pen for that. That way, hopefully, they will finish the school year with most of their stationery still in their possession. (Think of the money you'll save!)

Another great idea is to colour code their items for each different subject. For example, put red stickers or dots on all their English books, and blue dots or labels on their Maths books. That way they can just grab all the things with one particular colour before they head off for their lesson.

Organising folders

Purchase at least three really large A4 ring binder folders. Some students especially love this, as there is such a wide variety of funky, cool folders out there now. They could go for a colour scheme or a specific theme. There are tonnes to choose from these days. Once they have armed themselves with their large ring binders, they are ready to set them up.

Get your child to label one of the folders for three or four of their school subjects. For example: English, Social Studies and a language. We suggest using a coloured divider for each of these subjects, and make sure they put at least ten plastic sleeves behind each divider. That way, they always have one on hand to store any handouts they are given. If they have binder books for these subjects, pop these in too. Make sure they are named!

Their second folder should be labelled with the other subjects they are taking, such as Maths, Science and Biology. Organise this in the same way – dividers and plastic pockets.

Their third folder should be labelled 'Homework Folder'. We'll discuss how to use it effectively in the homework section of this book, on page 149. This folder approach is of particular assistance for those children who are prone to losing items, especially single worksheets and homework tasks.

TEACHERS

'Teachers open the door, but you enter by yourself.'
—*Chinese proverb*

I recall one particular teacher when I was growing up who, to put it nicely, I didn't click with. I didn't like much about her teaching style – she was a bit gruff and straightforward – and to be honest I also wasn't a fan of the subject, Accounting. It was my least favourite subject. The methods confused me and I just couldn't see myself heading down that career path. Nothing against Accounting. It just wasn't my thing.

Unfortunately, that teacher quickly became my least favourite teacher. And I must admit that, in retrospect, I didn't respond well either. I even had some fiery conversations with this teacher in my senior years at school. It's not that I didn't like her as a person. All that mattered to me as a student was that I hated the subject and her style and dreaded my lessons with her.

This experience will probably resonate with many parents reading this book, whether their children are in primary school or secondary school. A key message for parents to send their Year 7s is that teachers are not their mortal enemies and have not been placed on this earth to make their life a misery (although it might seem like that's the case sometimes).

The fact is that teachers are there to guide your child through their schooling and to help them learn and discover many things for themselves, not to force-feed them tonnes of useless information that they will never remember anyway. As with any relationship, there will be some teachers who they will warm to and some they will not. They will find it easier to relate to some teachers than others, and that's just a part of living within any community. (If they think their teachers are tough, wait until they get a boss.)

It's a bit like with an extended family – aunts, uncles and cousins. There are some family members who we get along with really well, and others we will just have to learn to at least tolerate. Parents need to remind their secondary schooler that teachers are people too, and they went through secondary school just like everyone else. They really do know what it's like to be a secondary school student and their job is to help your Year 7 learn, gain greater independence as a learner and discover things for themselves.

Tips for getting along with teachers

'Teachers are humans too. They are worth getting to know.'
—*Sharon Witt*

Show respect

Parents should stress that students should show respect for their teachers at all times. They may not always agree with them and they may not always feel like settling down and paying attention in class, but they do need to demonstrate a basic level of care and respect towards adults.

Listen

Listening is a learned skill and one that is very important during secondary school years. Remind your child that they will miss out on valuable information and instructions if they don't listen. It is also a sign of respect for their teacher. They can further demonstrate their attention by maintaining eye contact.

Seek further explanation

Your secondary schooler will not always understand everything that they see and hear in class. If they are unsure about some information or a task that needs to be completed, encourage your Year 7 to speak to their teacher about it, and to ask questions. If the teacher is too busy, encourage your child to arrange a suitable time to seek further clarification. Many secondary school teachers are more than happy to receive emails from their students, using their specific school address, as this allows them to answer at a time that suits them.

Never gossip about the teacher

Spreading gossip means talking about someone behind his or her back. It's all hurtful, no matter how trivial it may seem. Live by the rule to never say anything about someone that you wouldn't be comfortable saying to one's face. (See page 81 for more on the harm caused by gossip.)

If you or your child hear a rumour about a teacher, do not pass it on. If they do happen to hear some gossip about a teacher the best thing is to speak to someone else in authority, such as their class teacher or school counsellor. This also goes for online chatter on social media. Encourage your child to be the one who puts a stop to such gossip.

When you hear something about a teacher from your Year 7, remember that how your child perceives a teacher is often just that – their perception. Their emotions often relate to how they are feeling about themselves, their stress level, and what else might be happening in their life at the time.

Case study

Jackson arrived at school one morning after an emotional fight with a family member. Along the way, he realised he had left his English assignment at home on the kitchen bench in his haste to leave the house. Today was the deadline and he has already submitted work late once before.

The teacher was less than impressed. Jackson's response? It wasn't so good; he was angry at himself more than anyone, but he let his tension and anguish out on the teacher. In psychology, we call this projection. Instead of reflecting on his own actions, Jackson has someone to blame for his tension now: Mum, Dad, the teacher. He has now constructed a series of circumstances that leaves him feeling like no one cares.

The issue with the family member can be resolved at home. Jackson will work it through with encouragement or guidance from his parents. But what about the fallout with the teacher? Does Jackson bother to patch that relationship up? Does he go back later and explain himself and get the communication channel flowing again? And, most importantly, does he try to understand where the teacher is coming from, why there might have been some disciplinary action required to teach Jackson and the class a lesson?

Teachers aren't perfect. Neither are mums and dads. And here's the revelation – Year 7s are not exactly perfect, either.

What to do when they don't get along with their teacher

Unfortunately, schools, like parents, are never perfect, and not all teachers are perfect either. Sometimes, teachers are just not suited to the difficult task of guiding teenagers. Trust me, it's not an easy job.

If your Year 7 encounters a difficult teacher, or for some reason they just cannot get along with a teacher, there are some things to consider to help give some perspective and help your child manage this issue.

It's really important that they don't make it personal, even if they feel like the teacher is making it their mission to single them out and make their life a misery. Never let it become a personal vendetta, or draw other students together against a teacher. Your Year 7's experience is their experience, and they need to be mature about dealing with this issue. I am not saying to be silent or to assume it's all the student's fault all the time, but there is a right and a wrong way of dealing with a teacher/student clash.

Encourage your child to have a conversation with their pastoral care teacher, year level coordinator, school chaplain or welfare officer. If that doesn't help, or if you feel that it is an important enough issue, seek out a meeting with your school principal. Generally speaking, though, your child's year level coordinator should be able to offer valuable guidance and strategies to sort through issues they are having with a teacher.

Certainly, a teacher should never put your Year 7 down in front of other students (or when alone for that matter!). Nor should a teacher threaten or intimidate the student in any way. If your Year 7 feels that they are being picked on or victimised by a teacher, make sure they discuss how they feel with someone they trust. They may have to be taught by this teacher for a few years, so it's best to try and resolve any issues as early as possible. As a word of caution here, don't try and inflame the issue by being rude or disrespectful to the teacher concerned. It just doesn't help either student or parent.

Another word of caution for parents: please be aware that some students come home telling some of the story, while leaving out some of the more important elements of the scenario.

For example, Lucy may come home and tell her mother that her English teacher told her off for no reason at all, and made her move to the front of the classroom, away from her best friend Jessica. Lucy may express that her teacher is singling her out because she doesn't like her. She is being picked on!

If you were to have a respectful conversation with Lucy's English teacher (in person or via email), you may be surprised to hear that Lucy has received several verbal warnings in class about talking to Jessica while the teacher is giving instructions. Lucy has also been continually scribbling notes and passing these along to other students, distracting these other students from their learning.

After throwing a pen at another student, Lucy was eventually moved to the front of the classroom by her teacher to allow others to learn more effectively, and for Lucy to hopefully be less distracted and able to focus more effectively.

HOMEWORK

'I leave homework until the last minute because I will be older, therefore wiser.'
—*Unknown*

Homework is actually, seriously, really not a bad word! It may not be the most pleasant of tasks and yes, it might just get in the way of your Year 7's social life, but it's one of the necessary parts of secondary school. So let's deal with it!

Many students develop the habit of completing homework during their years of primary schooling, but many more don't. Unfortunately, it then becomes one of the major concerns and worries for many families entering secondary school.

The trick is to try not to stress out. Even if your Year 7 has never completed homework, all hope is not lost! The good news is that some easy homework skills can be learned, practised and then become a part of your child's everyday life. This will mean

easier completion of their homework tasks and therefore more time to do the things they want to . . . like anything that's not homework.

Ever wondered what happens in the staffroom during recess and lunch? Maybe the teachers huddle together and discuss ways to punish and annoy their students? Not exactly. Not even close.

Homework is not a conspiracy to destroy your child's life. There is much debate over whether setting homework for children is necessary, particularly in the first year of secondary school when there are a myriad of changes and stresses your child may already be navigating. Certainly, it is important that homework doesn't impose on important leisure and family time in the evenings. However, for many schools, homework is part and parcel of being a secondary school student. Here are the major reasons why homework is set.

Revision

Many teachers set small homework tasks by way of consolidating (making sure their students really understand) what has been completed during the day's lesson. You may have heard it said that practice makes perfect. That's quite true for many of the methods your child might learn for a subject, such as Maths, for example.

Just say your child has just been given a lesson in dental hygiene (brushing teeth). The teacher may discuss all the various reasons why it's essential that they brush and floss their teeth twice daily. The teacher may also demonstrate how to use the toothpaste and which way they should brush their teeth and at which angles. That could be all well and good, but unless they actually complete the task for themselves, and put into practice what they have been taught, they probably won't truly understand the value of the lesson.

Perhaps your child has been taught how to write paragraphs in English class. They may be set a homework task to complete paragraphs on a list of topic sentences. Now unless they go home and try to write some paragraphs for themselves, in their own time and away from classroom distractions, they may not know if they really understand how to properly construct them. So, homework really is, first and foremost, about practice and consolidation.

Developing study/organisation habits

Another entirely valid reason for homework is that it teaches your Year 7 student, hopefully, to set aside a regular time of day to complete set work for school. If done correctly, and they're well prepared, their homework shouldn't take them ages to complete. They will have one or two tasks that they might need to complete for homework each night. If they are organised, they should be able to finish them, mark them off their list and then relax for the rest of the evening, guilt free!

Learning to complete a task

The third valid reason for homework is that it allows Year 7 students a set time to complete unfinished tasks from school. Sometimes, they won't finish a piece of work in class due to distractions or lack of understanding. They should use 15–20 minutes of their homework time each evening to finish off any incomplete schoolwork that they have.

Learning to deal with procrastination

'The shortest way to do many things is to do only one thing at once.'
—*Samuel Smiles*

Procrastination is an ugly word. It means putting off doing something that we know we must do, but that we just can't seem to get started on. We find a million and one other things to do except the very thing that we should be doing. The funny thing is, if we just took the time to complete the task, we'd have it finished in much less time than it's taken us to keep putting it off. (Much like cleaning up their bedroom!)

Don't let your Year 7 leave their homework hanging over their head like a massive rain cloud. It won't actually go away, even if they pretend it's not there. They will just have more to complete the next night, and the next, and . . . you get the picture.

Instead, encourage them to set a time limit and a goal and get it done. Homework teaches them the valuable lesson of setting a task, then seeing it through to completion. They will feel a real sense of achievement when they do, and this is a lifelong skill to develop.

Q&A

How much homework should my Year 7 be completing each night?

This is a popular question among both parents and students! (More specifically, most students are asking, 'What is the minimum I have to complete?')

There is no definitive answer for this question as every school is different and each year level has different homework expectations. The following are merely guidelines – not the final word.

In their first year of secondary school, Year 7s are not expected to go like a bull at a gate and spend five hours at their work station each night, completing pages and pages of homework. I always say a useful guideline for the first year of secondary school is between 30-45 minutes per night. This is not to be confused with a statement like, 'I haven't done any homework for the past three weeks and now I have about 120 hours worth of homework and I'm only in Year 7.'

Homework expectations in secondary school usually increase each year. For the second year, students might be completing up to an hour each night and this may increase for the next few years. Usually, in their senior school years, particularly their final year, students will be expected to complete at least a couple of hours of homework each night. This is because they need to complete many more assignments and work requirements and there is much more study that needs to be completed for final exams.

Let's map it out

'The best way to get something done is to begin.'
—*Unknown*

Note, what follows is a guideline for completing a small amount of homework each evening. That way it shouldn't build up to an overwhelming state.

Imagine if your Year 7 has been set a history assignment on the Industrial Revolution and they have four weeks in which to complete it. It would be quite easy to see this assignment as a giant elephant – the task just seems so HUGE and overwhelming.

If they break it down into smaller, more bite-sized chunks, however, completing this mammoth task can become quite manageable. As the well-known saying goes: How do you eat an elephant? One bite at a time!

Week 1
- Break the assignment down into the major questions.
- Begin researching using online resources and books.
- Write a plan for structuring the assignment.

Week 2
- Write down notes under each of the major research questions.
- Complete research notes by the end of the second week.
- Type up Bibliography page, if one is required, listing all the resources used.

Week 3

- Collect any diagrams and pictures that will be used for the project.
- Write/type up rough draft of assignment.
- Have the rough draft proofread and checked for spelling and grammatical errors by the teacher or parent/caregiver. (Many teachers accept drafts of assignments for checking before the due date, so if your child's teacher makes this generous offer, make sure they utilise it!)

Week 4

- Type up the final copy of the assignment. Make sure to take note of any changes made by the proofreader.
- Add in illustrations and pictures.
- Design the front cover if there is one.
- Submit the assignment!

Note: Make sure your child thanks their 'proofreader'/parent/ guardian – they'll appreciate it and might even be willing to help out again next time.

Homework tips
General advice:

- Gently suggest that your Year 7 establishes a specific, designated area that they will be able to use to complete homework each night.
- Mobile phones and devices (with the exception of a laptop/ computer if required for a homework task) should be put away.

- Encourage your Year 7 to make sure they have the right tools they need (pens, paper, printer etc.).

- Encourage them to establish a routine: try to stick to the same time each night where possible – in my experience, routine soon becomes habit.

- Keep it simple. Remind them to try and complete simple and reasonable small homework tasks on the day they are set for each subject. That way, they won't build up and they are less likely to be forgotten.

- Suggest using a homework folder to carry work to and from school. That way, your child won't have to lug home ten folders and fifty textbooks. (There's more detail about this below.)

- Don't let your Year 7 procrastinate. Putting off work that needs to be done is the ultimate time waster – it just stresses them out anyway, so encourage them to sit down and get it done.

Setting up a homework folder

This is a fairly simple idea and one that I find helps many students organise their homework for ultimate success. They can use any type of ring binder or ordinary folder. It doesn't have to be a large, bulky one. Label it clearly as their 'Homework Folder'. Inside this folder, add about 10–15 plastic pockets. Your child may even like to go one step further and add individual subject dividers for each of the subjects they'll have homework set for. Make sure they also include loose-leaf lined paper in the folder to complete set work.

As students receive handouts or worksheets for homework, they can then simply pop these into the plastic pockets. Many textbooks now have online versions, so there is less pressure to have to lug them to and from school. There are even reasonably thin text-books that can actually slide into these plastic sleeves as well. This way, students really only need to take their homework folder home from school each day. Once your child has completed a piece of homework, they should place this into a plastic sleeve inside their folder so they won't misplace it before their next lesson.

Notices

To reach the ultimate in administrative organisation, your Year 7 can even go one step further and clearly label one of the plastic pockets in their homework folder as 'Notices'. This way, all their school notices can be placed in the same folder that goes home each day. Hopefully, the notices will then make it home safely to their parent or guardian.

As a side note, many schools are now moving into the digital space (and being environmentally conscious) by emailing notices and newsletters home to parents. If your child's school is using this method, ensure your email details are correct with the school administration. If your contact details change at any stage, alert the school office immediately. Other schools are now using online parent portals that allow parents to access all school communica-tion, including notices regarding excursions and camps etc.

Creating a homework space

Imagine that you have an appointment in the principal's office one day to discuss an issue regarding your Year 7. When you arrive at their office, you find papers lying everywhere, folders open all over the floor, and bits and pieces of what appear to be junk and lolly wrappers across the desktop.

'Wait a minute,' the principal exclaims. 'I can't find my glasses!'

You look away, laughing into your hand. Not only are the glasses on their head but they have also forgotten to replace their pyjamas with something more professional for the day's appointments.

What's wrong with this story?

Well, it's just not going to happen (hopefully!). Most principals will be ordered and well prepared. Their work space will be something more organised than what we have described here.

To give your Year 7 every chance of success, they need to set up a properly organised work station in your home. This doesn't need to be an expensive exercise. All they really need is a good sturdy table and a chair to sit on. (We'll cover some of the other essentials a little later on page 159.)

It would be ideal if this space was just for them, so that they have somewhere to go each night for a set time. In most homes, Year 7s may only have their bedroom, and perhaps they share their room with a sibling. If they choose to work in their room, try to make it as uncluttered as possible. It is also advisable not to have a TV or gaming station in the place where they study, because this can be a huge distraction. A section of the family room can be just as valuable, or if they are really lucky they might even have a separate study at home that they can use. Some students find it easier to work in a communal space such as at the dining room table. It's the same for adults: we know the conditions in which we work best, but we've learned this over time and through trial and error. Children need to be given the chance to work out which space will work best for them.

For me, I need to work in a space around people, which is why I write best in a coffee shop where I can be fed and watered at the same time as having bustling noise and conversations happening around me.

Some students tell us that they find it much easier to concentrate and complete their homework while having earphones on and listening to music. We can't deny this as an effective tool for some, as we know that different students require different study conditions. Our suggestion would be to observe what seems to work best for your child, and encourage them to use the method that is most successful. If they are procrastinating and far too distracted, insist on alternative conditions.

'Find a place for everything and you'll never have to go searching again.'
—*Sharon Witt*

Once your Year 7 has decided on a suitable location, they will need to make sure that they set up their homework space for maximum effect. Try to imagine you are setting up a work office (but you can have a bit of fun – you might want to choose a particular colour or theme). Basically, they'll need the following equipment at their work station so that they will be properly prepared.

Homework station equipment
- Spare lined paper
- Pens and pencils
- Whiteboard or corkboard (to record due dates for work, see page 163)

- Eraser and correction fluid
- Plastic pockets
- Large folder – their homework folder
- Calculator
- Computer/laptop (desirable, but not essential)
- Printer (if required)

Invalid homework excuses

- 'I had to clean my room.'
- 'We had visitors.'
- 'I forgot!'
- 'I left my gear at school.'
- 'The dog chewed it up and now I have to wait for it to come out!'
- 'We were visited by aliens and all they took back with them was my homework!'
- 'I thought it was due next week.'
- 'I couldn't find a pen.'
- 'My mum threw it out.'
- 'It got wet.'

Q&A time

What if months go by and my child still doesn't appear to have any homework set?

I hear you! The old 'I completed all my homework at school' line. Or better still, 'We don't get any.'

While it is quite possible that your child has finished off any small homework tasks during class time, or at the school library during their lunchbreak, the reality is that if you have not seen your Year 7 student do so much as a whiff of homework all term, it's time to be a little concerned. It is worthwhile sending an email to your child's year level coordinator to query if homework is indeed being set by subject teachers.

Firstly, it is quite an unlikely scenario that your child has escaped homework for an entire term. At the very minimum, there should be time spent reading their English novel or working on a research assignment. The point is not necessarily what is being set by teachers, it is the habit of setting aside a small window of time each school night to revise, complete tasks or read for thirty minutes.

Secondly, if your child is indeed not submitting set homework from teachers, you may expect them to sit a detention at school where the student gives up their own free time to complete work.

Not all teachers will set homework. This decision is usually left up to an individual teacher's discretion. But the last thing you want as a parent is to turn up to parent-teacher interviews to find out your child has been lagging behind in the homework department all term.

Many schools have moved into an online system of recording homework and assignments set for students in their own unique portal that is accessible by parents. This has enabled a vast improvement in the access parents are given to their child's learning. It allows them to see what requirements have been set by each of their child's teachers and what marks have been given throughout the term (without having to wait for end-of-term reports), and in general enables far greater communication between school and home. As a parent, it is your responsibility to engage fully with the system, if your child's school offers it. Your child's school may offer information nights to explain their system to parents, particularly for parents of Year 7 students, and most teachers are happy to help with any troubleshooting for parents still learning their way around it. If you haven't worked with an online school system before, it may appear a little daunting at the very beginning. But it's worth getting to know your way around such a system, as it can offer great support not only to your child, but also to you as a parent.

From my experience, those students that do best with establishing good organisation techniques and habits are those whose parents are on board with the school and are helping to keep their Year 7 accountable. I don't suggest you be a sergeant major and stand over your child while they complete their homework, but children do require guidance, particularly in those early days of secondary school when they need to develop good habits. So I would suggest that you regularly check what homework has been set, and that it has been done.

For the visual learners

Many children do well by having visual reminders so they can see the tasks ahead of them. A simple way of achieving this is by purchasing a small whiteboard that can be displayed easily above your child's desk. Rule this up into a grid with days of the week and spaces where homework tasks can be clearly recorded and ticked off when completed. Another helpful tip is for students to write key study notes on large poster paper and stick this onto their bedroom walls during study weeks.

A reward could even be listed under the day of the week after the task for the day is completed, e.g. thirty minutes of extra screen time, playing basketball for an hour, watching a TV show.

TESTS AND EXAMS

Your Year 7 may be tested from time to time by some teachers to gauge their level of understanding of different subjects. This assists the teachers in knowing what students have remembered and which areas they need to improve on. It also helps the teacher to make the lessons productive and effective.

Students are most likely to receive regular testing in the areas of Maths, Science and English. Encourage them to make use of any revision sheets provided by their teacher and to make time to revise before a test. However, inform your child that these tests don't determine whether they are a good student or not, or if they are 'smart'. They merely provide teachers with guidance as to whether your child is grasping the key concepts taught in class (and whether they are taking the time to revise for consolidation). Please reassure your child that they should not be concerned about tests that occur during their classes.

What the students have to say . . .

I wish my parents could understand that it's not all about getting the best scores; it's all about trying your very best. The only way to get better scores is to try your best and work hard. Giving maximum effort is very valuable.

Mia

Why do I need to know all this stuff?

This is a fairly common question among students. 'Why do I need to know all this information?' When I was studying Year 11 Accounting that's precisely what I was thinking.

'I'll never even use this stuff anyway,' I told my teacher. Well guess what!? Now, thirty years later, I am running my own publishing business and doing all my own accounts! So we just never know when or where we will draw on some of the things we are learning in school.

It's true that no Year 7 will be able to remember all of what they are learning in secondary school. But remember, it's not just what they learn, it's the process of being a learner. Learning skills such as listening, comprehension, writing, discussing, study skills – these are all valuable skills that they will use once they've completed their secondary school education. And, like me, you never know when you might use some of the knowledge you are picking up!

A word about NAPLAN

In Year 7, all students across the nation take part in the National Assessment Program – Literacy and Numeracy, more commonly known as NAPLAN tests. According to the Australian Curriculum

Assessment and Reporting Authority, NAPLAN is a national, consistent measure to determine whether students are meeting important educational outcomes. These take place at the same time for all students during the second term of the year, usually over a three-day period. These tests cover language, reading and maths.

Please assure your Year 7 that they should not worry about these tests. They will most likely have sat the same tests during primary school in Year 3 and Year 5, and will already be familiar with the format and processes. The results provide the school with valuable information as to what their students already know, and measure their ability levels in each of these areas. They are also used to help guide and support the students in their learning. In my opinion, some schools make a bigger deal of NAPLAN results than they ought to – informing prospective parents and proudly spruiking their results on their school website. (I recently heard of a school that opened an interview with prospective parents by referencing their impressive NAPLAN results. I would personally be more interested in the character of the students they are producing.) Schools can place far too much emphasis on preparing their students for these tests, causing the students undue stress. NAPLAN results only give an indication of how your child performed under the circumstances of that specific test on that particular day. Your child may be unwell on the day of one of the tests, or may have been unable sleep the night before. Perhaps they are experiencing anxiety.

NAPLAN results do not tell us what sort of student your child is. They can't tell us that your child is a good friend to others, or welcoming to new students, that they are a strong leader in group situations, that they have a vivid and creative imagination, or that they will offer to read out loud in class in front of their peers even though it makes them nervous. These results will not reveal that your child is always prepared for class or quietly thanks their teacher at the end of each lesson.

So while we encourage students to always try their best, including on their NAPLAN tests, the best advice you can give your Year 7 is that these results will not matter in one week, one year, or five years. Your child is not the sum of their test results.

Exams

Towards the end of the year your child will most likely sit exams. Each secondary school will have a different policy on when and how these take place, but it is likely that your child will begin exams from Year 7. They should try not to get too stressed out about exams in the early years of secondary school. While it's true that they do need to study for them and ensure they are well prepared, their results are not the 'be-all-and-end-all' assessment of their abilities. If their marks are not high, this does not mean they will automatically repeat the school year. Schools take many factors into consideration before recommending a student repeat a year.

Once they move into the latter years of secondary school – Years 10 to 12 – there is certainly a greater emphasis placed on final exam results. And in Years 11 and 12, these exam results will form part of their overall grade, or ATAR score.

Exam time can be quite stressful for many students. It needn't be! There are many useful tips and pieces of advice that can help them prepare well for their exams and allow them to deal with stress when they are feeling a bit overwhelmed. We'll discuss some of these in the pages that follow.

Remember too that not all stress is bad. While it is often given a bad rap, the right amount of stress can actually motivate your Year 7 to get stuff done. Many people work best when there is a deadline ahead of them. Deadlines, as much as they annoy us, often prove to be very motivating. The improved motivation as a deadline looms can be explained to some extent by the Yerkes-Dodson law, originally developed in 1908, which argues that performance increases as arousal increases, but only up to a point. After that point, performance starts to suffer as the person becomes overwhelmed or distracted. The key is to recognise when stress has tipped over from being a motivating force to an overwhelming emotion. A little stress can be good for your Year 7 and can improve the efficiency of their performance. Ultimately, if they have too little stress this can lead to boredom and depression, while an excess of stress can cause anxiety and poor health.

Study tips for exams
Routine

Encourage your child to set a regular timeframe when they will study each night and to stick to it. It's important that their study time becomes a habit.

Study space

As outlined previously in our advice about setting up for homework success, it's really important that your child's study space is both comfortable and well lit. Don't allow them to sit on the couch to study. Ensure they sit at a desk where their study time is purposeful.

Say it out loud

One of the best ways for your Year 7 to really remember and learn is to talk about what they are learning out loud, without any notes. In 2017 MacLeod and Bodner's research on the 'production effect' looked at people's memory for things like a list of words. They asked half their participants to study the list by reading the words silently and the other half to say the words out loud. The words spoken aloud were remembered much better than those that were read silently. Another study, by Atkins, found that we are far better at problem solving when we think out loud, making 78 per cent fewer mistakes than if we silently puzzle things over in our heads.

Establish a timetable

When your child is studying for a series of tests or exams, it's helpful to get them to draw up a study timetable to ensure that they dedicate specific time to each subject. This is where a whiteboard can be useful so that your child has a visual reminder to block out study periods for different subjects. This can be especially helpful for those who respond well to visual cues.

The twenty-minute rule

No one can study for six hours straight and still be effective. As parents, we should encourage our Year 7s to break up their time into twenty-minute chunks. On average, the Year 7 brain is not designed to remain focused on a single task for a significantly long time – most students usually begin to lose focus and concentration after twenty minutes. Their quality of reception starts to drop and their ability to adequately grasp information from their point of attention deteriorates. At this point, their brain requires some time off, a distraction. So get your child to schedule mini-breaks every twenty minutes to keep their attention up.

Look after their health

It's difficult to study on an empty stomach or when you have no energy. Make sure your Year 7 drinks lots of water while trying to avoid too many caffeinated drinks, such as coffee and Coke. Have lots of healthy snacks on hand (nuts are a great source of energy) and encourage them to exercise regularly. Make sure that they take short breaks at specific times during their study timetable, when they could go for a walk or do some other physical activity. Even during exam time, we encourage young people to keep up with their regular sporting commitments. These provide a much-needed physical break from study and also help get a dose of those feel-good endorphins released through physical exertion.

Sleep

We've already discussed the importance of sleep to teenagers' health and, as I mentioned earlier, sleep is the most important study tool going around. Your Year 7 won't retain any information if they are dog tired, so if it's late or they are just plain exhausted, encourage them to go to bed! They can always set their alarm and get up early in the morning to catch up.

Avoid interruptions

When your child is in study mode, try to avoid things like having the computer and internet on (social networking sites can be killer timewasters!). That'll protect them from being distracted by messages constantly popping up. The same goes for their mobile phone – make sure it is switched off or out of the room when they are studying. We suggest the use of free programs like Cold Turkey (https://getcoldturkey.com), which can help your Year 7 reclaim their free time and boost their productivity by blocking time-wasting websites and applications.

A good idea is to let the whole family know what the Year 7 study timetable is, by posting a copy somewhere communal like on the fridge, and make it a family rule not to disturb your child during their study periods if possible.

Remain calm

There isn't a great deal of purpose in your child stressing themselves out. They can only do what they can do, so the best cure for stress is to do something about what's causing them stress. That might just be preparing for the exams. When they need to take a break, suggest that they try lying down somewhere peaceful and listening to some calming music or a meditation app. Let the music or guided imagery take them away.

Set rewards

As with any goals, parents can establish some mini rewards for when their child takes study breaks. For example, they could watch something on YouTube or a favourite TV show, catch up with friends, play some sport or watch a favourite movie.

Ask for help

If they are unsure about any part of their subject matter, make sure your child seeks out their teacher and asks for clarification – that's what their teachers are there for! Their peers can also be another great help. Encourage your child to ask a classmate for help if they are struggling. They can always repay the favour by offering to help them in another subject.

Find a study buddy

A study partner can be really helpful for your Year 7, especially if they are studying for a subject that they are having trouble with. Peer tutoring can be one of the most beneficial ways to understand parts of a subject that you're struggling with. Often when a friend or classmate explains something in their own language, this can help your child to understand it better. Suggest that your child finds a classmate, or perhaps an older student, who can offer help in studying. They can then do the same in return: if they are really great at English, for example, they could offer to help someone else who struggles with this subject area. A word of warning here, though – you have to be really strict if your child is going to get a study buddy. It can be easy to get distracted by chatting about other stuff when they are together. A study partner might be best used for only one or two subjects.

Exam tips
Fuel up

Your Year 7 won't be able to perform at their best if they haven't fuelled their body properly. Ensure they have had a good feed before their exam – cereal, yogurt, eggs, blueberries, fish oil and avocado are all excellent brain foods. Make sure they also have a bottle of water to hydrate them during their exam. And if their exam is in the morning, make sure they have had a good, healthy breakfast.

Get a good night's sleep

The night before their exams, make sure your child gets a good night's sleep! They have studied all they can (hopefully), and even if they haven't, cramming the night before won't make too much difference. There's nothing left to do but get a good, solid night's rest. Their brain will thank them for it in the morning!

Read the entire exam paper first

There was a funny joke played on students once (not during exams though!) in which the first instruction on the paper was to read the entire test paper first before writing anything down. Clearly, not all students did as they were asked, as many spent the entire hour of their test busily concentrating and writing. Those that did read the entire test first actually finished in about five minutes flat and sat there smiling, looking very satisfied with themselves. Why? Because the very last question on the test paper said, 'Ignore all other questions and complete only number 1'!

Once your Year 7 has read the entire exam questions, they can then plan how much time they should allocate to each question and section of the exam and make sure that they are not surprised by anything at the last minute.

Complete all the questions

This might sound obvious, but many students simply leave a question if they don't know the answer. Even if they are unsure, they should at least give the question a go. One mark or even half a mark received can be the difference between a pass and a fail.

Be prepared

Make sure your child arrives at their exam with the appropriate equipment. They will need at least two pens – an extra one in case a pen runs out – a pencil, a calculator and an eraser. They won't be able to ask someone for a pen midway through the exam!

Plan their exam time

As soon as the student has read carefully through their exam, they should write a quick exam schedule on a piece of scrap paper so that they can allocate a set amount of time for each section. This will help ensure that they don't leave themselves short on time for completing the final section.

TAKEAWAYS FROM THIS SECTION

- Organisation is key

  Take the time from the get go to ensure your secondary schooler has all the books and stationery they will require to give them the best chance of success. Check in with them regularly to see if they need any items replaced.

- Develop positive relationships with teachers
  Teachers are such an important part of your child's secondary school experience. Trust them and encourage your child to develop a respectful relationship with them. Speak well about your child's teachers (even when you may personally disagree with them). Communicate with your child's teachers and identify any issues early on so that they can be resolved quickly.

- Monitor and manage devices and online activity
  Devices should be a privilege, not a right. Ensure your secondary schooler doesn't simply have free rein over their devices and the internet. Monitor their use and ensure they have plenty of time designated away from being online or on devices.

- Insist they complete a small amount of homework each night
  Completing homework each night needn't be a burden to students (or their parents) if a small amount is consistently planned for and completed each evening. The problems generally occur when there has been a pattern of ignoring homework and then suddenly everything that has been left to the last minute is due at once. Be present for your child as they are completing their homework, however, don't do it for them!

Part 4

Help is at hand

STRUGGLING WITH SCHOOLWORK

Sometimes, your Year 7 will have trouble understanding a subject.

The truth is, some areas of school just seem to suit some students better than others. I personally really struggled with Maths and Accounting during secondary school – I just didn't get it! It may have been partly due to my teachers' explanations, but I now recognise that I also often tuned out when it got difficult. I was in a whole other world. This is not helpful, of course. Tuning out is not a great response to a lack of understanding.

Ask for help!

I never understood fractions in Maths. I just never got it! The explanations offered by my Maths teachers just added to my confused state. It wasn't long before I was a teacher myself, and guess what subject I was given in my first year of teaching? You guessed it . . . Maths. I was forced to ask a fellow teacher to explain exactly how fractions worked. Bingo! I understood his explanation immediately. 'Is that all?' I remember asking.

Sometimes it might require a teacher to explain it to your Year 7 one-on-one, or another student to have a go, before the penny drops and they understand the concepts. Maybe they can ask a parent, family friend or sibling who is good at that particular subject. The point is, make sure your Year 7 understands that they should not be afraid to ask. They will never get in trouble for asking for help!

WHEN SCHOOL ISN'T WORKING FOR YOUR CHILD

It is true that secondary school doesn't work out for everyone. This can be for a variety of reasons – lack of stimulating programs; inability to concentrate; or your Year 7's individual learning style might clash with their teachers.

Some students will struggle through the first few years of secondary school before they finally reach an age where they are able to leave school and gain work or start an apprenticeship. But it's a legal requirement to attend at least some of secondary school, so if it's not working too well for your child this can really make life difficult.

Attendance

This may seem like a really obvious point to make, but it must be said. Your Year 7 actually needs to attend secondary school! Not only is it a legal requirement but they need to attend in order to give themselves the very best chance of being successful at school. Many teachers have explained that one of the biggest factors in a student's success at secondary school is simply whether they turn up or not.

You see, if they get into the habit of taking regular days off, they miss important pieces of information and instructions that are often difficult to catch up on second-hand. There will be times when it's just not possible to attend school, for example if they are ill or there are other major problems. This makes it even more important to attend at other times. Taking regular days off, however, because they don't feel up to it (or are overtired because they've been staying up late watching Netflix or playing online games) will not cut it in the long run.

Your child only needs to miss a couple of days to really fall behind. If you can possibly help it, make sure they turn up to school, even when they just don't feel like it. If they do happen to miss a day, it is their responsibility to seek out the teachers they missed seeing and find out about any work missed and homework that needs to be completed. Sometimes, they can miss a few days and then get stuck in a rut because they fall further and further behind. That's not helpful for them.

Their best chance of success at secondary school is to make sure they attend.

Attitude

Sometimes, how a student is feeling about a situation actually comes down to their attitude. It may be more about what they are saying to themselves about each situation, and the negative language and explanations they use for their life at the moment – self-talk, remember (see page 39)!

For example, each time they go to a Science class, they might say to themselves, 'I hate Science', or 'It's the most boring subject in the world'! Well they probably will find that lesson incredibly boring, given that attitude.

Instead, encourage them to try this: next time they go to a Science class, suggest that they say to themselves, 'I find it difficult to understand Science sometimes but today I'm going to really try to concentrate and ask as many questions as I can. I'm going to participate in this class as if it were my last Science lesson.' They just might come away feeling a lot more positive about that lesson than they would have otherwise. Suggest they try it, there is nothing to lose.

I often hear Year 7 students saying things like, 'School sucks' or, 'I really hate Maths'. They will create their own reality by their thoughts and behaviours. When they are in a negative frame of mind, it can't help but affect what then occurs. I can't emphasise enough how important it is that they try and remain positive. They need to try faking it 'til they make it! In other words, pretending they actually like school until things turn around!

Peer groups

Sometimes Year 7s won't enjoy their secondary school experience because of particular peer groups or a lack of friends. This can be really difficult. In my professional experience, friendship and peer groups rate as one of the most important contributing factors for enjoying secondary school. My best advice in this case is to get out there and try to make friends. They might say, 'Well I've already tried that and it's just not working for me. I have no friends.' Then parents need to respond by saying something like, 'That may be your present circumstance, that might be what you're feeling right now, but there are things you can do to try and change this. Have you tried joining a group or club within the secondary school?' For example, they could try joining the student council or leadership group, the school band, the choir, the debating team, or a sports team. The list is pretty endless, but the point is that these groups can be a place where new friendships are formed.

When I ran a student council group with secondary school students, I commonly heard that students often discovered new people they had never known before. New friendships and social groupings can often be born out of joining a school club, so don't write that avenue off!

Communication

If your child tries some of the above strategies and is still feeling like school is just not working for them, it's important that they share their concerns with someone. That might be the year level coordinator or school welfare officer. Sometimes, a wise adult with knowledge of their situation and the school environment can give them some further strategies to consider that they might not have thought of before. The most important thing is for them to talk about it. Remember, they are not the only students who have had difficulty liking school, and they won't be the last!

WHEN SCHOOL *REALLY* ISN'T WORKING FOR YOUR CHILD

Sometimes, for any number of reasons, the secondary school that your Year 7 attends may just not be working for them. Maybe they have tried and are not able to form friendship groups. Perhaps the school is just not the right fit for them.

I am not saying that you should consider changing schools at the first hint that your Year 7 does not like the place because, for many students, there will come a point at which they just aren't enjoying their secondary school experience. For most, these feelings soon pass.

But for a small minority of students, their chosen secondary school just doesn't seem to fit, no matter how much they try. In some circumstances, a student might need to make a change or a fresh start at a new secondary school. This decision shouldn't be taken lightly, but it should be one that is made with your full support, as their parents.

If this is your Year 7 right now, and they really hate their secondary school environment, there are a few steps you, and they, ought to take. Start by talking to their year level coordinator or school counsellor. Even if they do end up leaving the school, there might be some valuable advice they could pass on to you or your child.

Before making any decision, however, it is worth visiting some other schools that might better suit the educational and social needs of your child. Don't shy away from discussing why it is that you are seeking a new school for your child. The last thing you want is to have a new start at another school and have the same issues be reignited. For example, if your child was bullied at a previous school, ensure that this is raised at any potential enrolment interview. Remember, schools can only work with the information you as parents provide them.

Case study

Liz decided to move her daughter, Monique, out of mainstream school by Term 3 of Year 7. Monique was extremely exhausted, possibly due to hormonal changes, and she was also experiencing some minor bullying by one of her three friends from Year 6. Mostly, this girl was degrading her friends but it became very consistent and then started to become physical. The teacher dealt with it well but, as a result, Monique began avoiding spending any one-on-one time with this girl. As the bullying only came to light at the very end of Year 6, the four girls had already selected possible classmates for Year 7. This resulted in Monique being in a class with the bully. Liz requested a change but that only resulted in Monique ending up with a choice between the class with the bully and a class with no friends. She chose the class with no friends and found the first half of the year really difficult. When all of that combined with Monique's anxiety and tiredness over winter, Liz knew they were all heading down a dangerous road. She ended up homeschooling Monique. Moving her out of mainstream schooling was a great decision. Monique now follows her passions and is so much more confident in her abilities, and she has a much clearer idea about where she wants to go in life.

It's not always a bad thing to change schools. When I was halfway through secondary school, my parents moved me to another secondary school, which they felt would better meet my educational needs. (It was a much more academically rigorous school and they thought I needed a kick in the toosh!) Even though it was not my choice at the time, as it turned out, my parents really did know what was best for me and the move to another school was very beneficial.

The most important thing to consider here is communication. Often, communicating any issues as soon as they become apparent can lead to small changes that may alter the situation and help your child become better settled in their secondary school. If you do make the decision together that a change of secondary school will be beneficial to your child, consider your Year 7's needs and seek out the best fit for them.

I always advise that it's worth ensuring that all other options have been considered at their present school. It's definitely best to try and leave a school on good terms. I have seen quite a few students change schools when they feel that another school is better suited to them, only to realise months down the track that it is, in fact, no better. There is always the option of returning to their previous school if things are left on good terms. In my experience as a teacher, sometimes students have felt the 'grass is greener' at another secondary school, only to realise later that what they had at their previous school was pretty great. They return with quite a different attitude.

For some students, changing to a secondary school that better suits their needs (such as providing greater sporting opportunities or specialisation in subjects like drama etc.) can be a positive outcome.

HELPING YOUR CHILD ON THE AUTISM SPECTRUM NAVIGATE SECONDARY SCHOOL

Transitioning into secondary school can be hard enough for young people, let alone for those who have added challenges to grapple with. For those parents with children on the autism spectrum, there is often the added stress of wondering how your child will cope in an entirely new environment (when it has often been such a long journey getting them acclimatised to the day-to-day mechanics of primary school).

The most important and obvious advice is to make sure you get a diagnosis, which will support the school's understanding of your child's needs and potentially help you with extra funding for support at school. To get an accurate diagnosis, connect with your local online autism parenting group and ask lots of questions to find out who are the best professionals in your area. Remember, while not all young people with autism are the same, as a group many do learn differently. Communication with the school is crucial so be proactive and always feel confident about getting a second opinion if you are not happy.

Many secondary schools now have specific special education coordinators and assigned learning assistants to help ease children on the autism spectrum into the new environment of secondary school. However, it is important for parents to be aware that they shouldn't simply assume that the school, and associated teachers, will all be on board to cater for the specific needs of your child. As much as we would like to think this may be the case, the reality is that your child is most likely going from a primary school of perhaps a few hundred students to a secondary campus with up to one thousand (or more) students in each year level.

I am sure this sounds daunting enough for you as a parent, let alone for your child, who needs extra support and reassurance. This is where you, as your child's advocate, are most important. You will be that voice for your child in a secondary school that is often very busy and loud.

Organise additional transition visits

During the latter part of Year 6, your child will take part in a transition program to familiarise themselves with their new secondary school. This will most likely involve an entire day spent at the school, attending a few taster classes in different subjects, learning the layout of the school, meeting teachers and other new Year 7 students. For a child on the autism spectrum, this is a LOT to take in over the course of one day. They are highly likely to be overwhelmed at receiving so much new information, as well as by the unfamiliar environment. For this reason, it is highly recommended that you organise an additional three or four visits to the secondary school during the second half of Year 6. This could be coordinated by your child's primary school teacher, but may also be facilitated by the secondary school through the special needs coordinator, head of wellbeing or assistant principal. My recommendation is to try and organise as many visits as possible. Each visit will provide familiarity for your child and assist in easing their anxiety about what to expect at secondary school. It will also allow them to prepare themselves for the different subjects and try new activities as well as familiarising them with the classrooms they will be expected to attend. Remember, your child will be used to the structure of primary school, where they have one class teacher and spend a great deal of time in the one classroom in a highly structured environment.

Overall, you want to provide a soft start for your child if they are on the autism spectrum. Secondary school can be a huge trigger for anxiety in children with additional needs. More practice and familiarity can be of great benefit.

Case study

Jack was diagnosed with Asperger's syndrome and was entering Year 7 at his co-educational school, which went from Prep–Year 12. This meant that he was already familiar with the primary school structure and environment, having been there for all of his schooling thus far. However, Jack had often seen the secondary Science teacher at school assemblies and other events within the school, and was quite afraid of this particular teacher due to his unfamiliar accent. Jack was quite concerned and anxious about having Science class with this man, despite the teacher being very friendly and well-liked by students.

To create a smooth transition, Jack was gently introduced to the new teacher at their first class and then took his place at the back of the science room. For the first few lessons Jack sat with his homeroom teacher at the back of the room. This allowed Jack to be present in Science class and see and listen to the teacher without it being too threatening for him. He then attended a few more lessons over coming weeks, accompanied by either his homeroom teacher or a learning assistant. Over a few weeks, Jack became familiar with his new teacher and his different accent, and before too long was more than happy to go off to Science class each week without any anxiety or fear.

What the above case study emphasises is that familiarity and time are the key for many students on the autism spectrum. A situation that may be slightly uncomfortable for us as parents, such as beginning a new job or having a new boss take over at work, can be ten times more difficult for a child with autism. By thinking outside the box and putting a plan in place, you can often make life much easier for your child. If there are any issues you know will be challenging for your child, ensure that you have a conversation with their coordinator about how a plan may be put in place well before the first day of secondary school.

Executive function challenges

For children on the autism spectrum, executive function challenges (the ability to plan, order, and carry out tasks) such as being organised, remembering what to bring to class and what needs to come home in the schoolbag can add to the stress of secondary school. It is helpful for parents to seek advice from an occupational therapist within the school community. They can help you and your child to develop helpful strategies for getting organised, particularly in the cases of children with extreme executive functional challenges. For a child with executive function challenges, being organised does not come naturally or easily to them and can be a source of endless frustration – both for the child themselves and for you as their parent. An occupational therapist can help your child develop organisational capacity, that is, they are able to use many strategies and tools to find what works best for them to help them be organised.

For children on the spectrum, the following skills and strategies can be particularly helpful to practise, and hopefully develop greater confidence in, before beginning secondary school:

- Packing their own bag for school the night before, with a visual prompt to get their lunch box from the fridge and pack it into their schoolbag in the morning before departing.
- Use of visual reminders, charts and checklists to help remind your child of things to remember to pack for school.
- Use of an alarm clock to be able to get themselves up and dressed for school each morning.
- Use of a school diary in the final year of primary school (this will then be one less thing to learn in secondary school).
- Colour coding of school books. For a child who struggles with organisation, secondary school doesn't make it easier with the increase in the amount of textbooks and binder books students are expected to lug around. Colour coding books by different subjects is a simple method for your child to identify which books to bring to which class. For example, use red dots for any English-related books, blue dots for Science, and yellow dots for Maths. All your child needs then is a visual key, which can be glued into their school diary or stuck to the inside of their school locker to remind them which books need to go with them to a particular class.

Case study

Ben, aged 12, is on the autism spectrum and has struggled with organisation and executive function. In his first year of secondary school this has been a particular problem when it comes to preparing equipment and books for specialist classes. Throughout the year, Ben has been the object of teacher's criticism for forgetting books and other items when he arrives to class, which has then ostracised him from his peers. Socially, this has resulted in Ben being labelled as 'dumb'. The major breakdown occurred because over half of his teachers were not made aware that he was on the autism spectrum and that a key issue was organisation. This resulted in punishments instead of understanding of his difficulties. As a result of increased frustration on both ends, Ben was yelled at by teachers. On one occasion, after being yelled at in front of the entire class, Ben yelled back at the teacher, swearing and pushing his chair backwards. As a result, he was given a three-day suspension.

There is no doubt that this situation would not have escalated to such a degree had Ben's teachers been made aware of his specific difficulties. The end result of his frustrated outburst may well have been avoided by:

1. Communication between all staff, so they were on board
2. Understanding of Ben's organisational challenges
3. The teacher giving him an additional opportunity to go back and get his books without drawing negative attention to him and embarrassing him in front of his peers.

Allow regulation and down time

Regulation and down time is all about providing a balance to the pressures of secondary school, as well as giving your child's mind and body some reprieve. For your Year 7 on the autism spectrum it is especially important that activities that bring them joy are built into their week. These may include dancing, drawing, music or gaming. It's also important that activities that constitute 'heavy work' (an activity that pushes or pulls against the body) are also incorporated into their weekly, if not daily, schedule. Any activities that use all the core muscles can help to reduce anxiety. You can encourage any activity that uses pressure, such as:

- Jumping on a trampoline
- Going for a walk
- Going for a run
- Any activity that requires pushing or pulling
- Bike riding
- Climbing
- Wrestling (under supervision)
- Big, strong hugs (if they allow this)
- Tight squeezes from Mum or Dad

Ensure that every teacher is aware of your child's ASD diagnosis

While you hope that every teacher who will encounter your child during their secondary school experience will have received a detailed file on your child's autism spectrum diagnosis and the specific requirements that will help ensure a smooth transition for each class, this is sadly not always the case. This is not because of lack of care from teachers. The simple fact is that your child may be one of a thousand new students in the secondary school, many with varying degrees and types of special support required. So the best thing you can do is be your child's greatest advocate as they begin their secondary school experience. Any formal information about your child's diagnosis, testing results, and documented strategies that have been adopted by previous teachers in primary school can be invaluable for new teachers, especially if your child does not receive any formal funding. However, again, please be realistic. If there are over a thousand Year 7 students and thirty or more with special learning needs, this could very well be a great deal of information for teachers to read through and process. Anything you can do to provide simple guidelines and strategies for teachers can help ease the process for your child. As teachers, we can only act on the information we have.

Regular emails (not demanding) to your child's teachers can be really helpful in keeping the lines of communication open, especially when it comes to homework and other work requirements. If your child is part of a supportive team that involves the parent, teacher, special education support staff and themselves, they have a much higher chance of success.

Many schools organise a document called 'All About Me' or something similar that is passed on to the specific teachers in secondary school to allow them to get to know new students. This provides a valuable framework for your child to communicate their strengths and challenges. If your child's school hasn't organised this, these documents are also available at www.spectrumjourneys.org.au.

All behaviour is communication

Be observant and look for changes in behaviour with your Year 7 that could indicate issues at secondary school, in particular, bullying. Many kids on the spectrum are not able to 'join the dots' in order to recognise behaviour towards them as bullying. This can be due to some children with autism having a literal interpretation, or a trusting nature. Some children will often accept the narrative that is given by the bully regarding their behaviour, such as that they are 'just joking' or 'we're just having fun'.

This is why it can be important to break things down with your child about their day.

- Who did they play with?
- What did they do at recess?
- Did anything worry them?

Behaviour is often the key indicator that something is not going well for your child at secondary school. This can include:

- Withdrawal
- Aggression
- Increased tiredness
- Avoidance of any form of demand
- Anxiety symptoms such as stomach aches, headaches and nausea
- School refusal

Communicating any concerning events involving your child to their homeroom teacher or year level coordinator as soon as you become aware of them is important, even if it doesn't entirely make sense to you. Often events recalled by your child can be like parts of a jigsaw puzzle that may need to have several pieces presented in order to get a full picture of the situation.

Finally, remember that you are the best support and advocate for your child as they begin and continue their secondary school experience. They can thrive with the right supports and structures in place so the more preparatory work you can do before they begin, the better. Continue to encourage them and watch them shine. (See 'Resources', page 219, for specific resources for your ASD child.)

MENTAL HEALTH

At the end of 2018 I was invited to launch the Mission Australia 2018 Youth Survey. This survey has been taking the psychological temperature of young Australians for over fifteen years and in 2018 was completed by more than 28 000 young Australians. The 2018 results showed a 10 per cent increase in concerns around mental health since the previous year. Another relevant finding was that four in ten (43 per cent) young people identified mental health as the top issue facing Australia today – up from 33 per cent in 2017 and doubling since 2016.

Mental health also entered the top three issues of personal concern in the annual survey. The top three personal concerns were coping with stress (identified as the top concern of 43 per cent of respondents), school or study problems (34 per cent) and mental health (31 per cent). In previous years, the third most cited item was body image (30 per cent), which moved to the fourth spot in 2018. Each of the top four personal concerns have strong links to mental health.

The survey highlights the importance of Year 7 parents listening to young people's clear and growing concerns around mental health and taking immediate action to ensure all young people have access to the right supports. Unfortunately, we know that help is not always there. The service system is difficult to navigate and the support offered can be patchy, especially outside of metro areas, and is often not tailored to the needs of young people and their help-seeking preferences. This has to be tackled as a priority.

New data released by the Australian Bureau of Statistics shows that the national suicide rate has increased over twelve months, from 11.8 deaths per 100 000 in 2016 to 12.7 deaths per 100 000 in 2017. This exceeds the World Health Organization's global average suicide mortality rate of 10.5 deaths per 100 000. The key message for Year 7 parents is to understand the connection between mental health problems and suicide. Preliminary data showed that 43 per cent of people who died by suicide in 2017 were living with a mood disorder (like depression), 29.5 per cent with a drug and alcohol use disorder, and 17.5 per cent with anxiety. From previous research by the Australian Bureau of Statistics, we know that people living with a complex mental illness are 13–45 times more likely to take their own life than those living without mental illness. That's why it's so important that the mental health and suicide prevention sectors work together.

The suicide rate for young men seems to have plateaued and is now showing the signs of decline. Sadly, in contrast, the suicide rate for young women, although much lower, has doubled since 2008. While this is tragic and disheartening, we have to admit that it comes as no great shock. Over the past decade, an increasing number of studies and reports document an evident and abrupt decline in teenage girls' mental health. From a clinical point of view, there have never been as many young women so stressed and so depressed, so early in adolescence.

We cannot ignore the fact that, for an increasing number of Australian girls, the journey through adolescence is manifestly miserable and that the transition from primary school to secondary school is a pivotal time for them.

Young people with mental health problems do less well in school than those without mental health problems, and are more likely to abuse alcohol and other drugs, engage in bullying behaviours both on- and offline and attempt suicide. It is not news to anyone in the mental health sector that anxiety and depression are two of the leading causes of the deteriorating mental health of young people in this country. This is a much-needed alarm for parents and doctors to look into the signs of depression and anxiety among young people, so that appropriate services can be provided on time. This is everyone's problem.

For the vast majority of mental health problems in young people, onset occurs by 24 years of age, with half of the occurrences beginning before the age of 15. Put simply, adolescence is a giant petri dish in which the seeds are sown for either a good mental health trajectory or a really lousy one. Which way a child develops is due to a mixture of genetics, personality, temperament, upbringing and the delicate balance of risk and protective factors in their environment.

The most crucial warning signs of mental distress or illness are social withdrawal, loss of interest in things that used to be pleasurable, trouble sleeping, decreased appetite and/or changes in energy levels. These behaviours may be a temporary response to a minor setback, such as a particularly bad week, a romantic break-up or not making the netball team. However, if they last longer than a couple of weeks and impact on your child's ability to function normally, these behaviours are more likely to be important and your Year 7 might require help to deal with their mental health.

A major challenge is encouraging young people to seek help, as illustrated by a 2015 UK study by the National Union of Students. Of the 1 093 students in further and higher education who were surveyed, 78 per cent said they experienced mental health issues in the last year, and over half of these students said they did not seek support. A third said they would not know where to get mental health support at their college or university if they needed it, and 40 per cent reported being nervous about the support they would receive from their institution.

Anxiety

Thirty years ago, anxiety disorders such as obsessive-compulsive disorder or generalised anxiety disorder in young people were almost

WORDS... WILL... NEVER... HURT... ME...
YEAH, RIGHT!

unheard of. Now, it's common: the 2013–14 University of Western Australia 'Young Minds Matter' survey showed that the rate of anxiety for young people aged 12–17 years was 6.9 per cent, and was more common in females (7.7 per cent compared to 6.3 per cent in males).

The functional nature of anxiety may be one reason for its increase. Human beings actually need a certain amount of stress or arousal to motivate us to give our best performance. If approached in the street by a mugger, for example, the anxiety we feel (the 'fight or flight response') enables us to react quickly to protect ourselves. A manageable level of anxiety about end-of-year exams, or an upcoming race or sporting competition, has been shown to be useful in enhancing our performance (as discussed on page 167).

Anxiety is a normal response to something that is terrifying or complicated. Adrenaline flows into the bloodstream, priming muscles, focusing attention, flooding the body with oxygen and releasing chemicals that transform the sugar in the bloodstream into energy. This is the body's response to perceived threat or danger and it happens to everyone if they are faced with a difficult situation. Originally named for its ability to enable us to physically fight or run away when faced with danger, this anxiety response is now activated in situations where neither response is appropriate, such as being stuck in traffic or during a stressful day at work. Anxiety is best understood as a cognitive false alarm. When the perceived threat is gone, systems are designed to return to normal functioning via the relaxation response, but in times of chronic stress this fails to happen often enough, causing damage to the body. The bottom line is that some Year 7s can get caught in fight or flight mode, and anxiety can start to take over their lives.

Anxiety warning signs

- Feeling a constant sense of dread that something terrible will happen
- Having trouble falling asleep
- Having difficulty concentrating or thinking straight
- Experiencing physical symptoms such as nausea, chest pain, involuntary shaking, increased sweating, difficulty breathing, racing heart (panic attacks)
- Exhibiting avoidance behaviours (any actions to escape or sidestep fearful thoughts and challenging feelings), or repetitive or obsessive behaviours

What to do

Engage your Year 7 in conversation: 'Do you ever feel like your heart is going to jump out of your chest or that you can't breathe?' or 'Do you ever feel that something terrible is going to happen even when you are safe?' Listen carefully to what they say. If they have had panic attacks, or are starting to feel a constant sense of dread even when they are 'safe', it's important to get professional face-to-face help. Take them to your GP and arrange to see a psychologist trained in cognitive behavioural therapy (which has a good success rate for anxiety treatment, according to a review by Kaczkurkin and Foa in 2015). If they don't get help, your child may eventually become so anxious about being anxious that they won't leave home in case they can't cope with their anxiety in public. This is panic disorder.

Some practical ways for you to help your child are to:

- Find out everything you can about anxiety
- Encourage your child to exercise and to avoid caffeine and sugar (they activate the fight or flight response)
- Practise deep breathing or diaphragmatic breathing with them
- Try the online 'Brave' program, developed by Beyond Blue and the University of Queensland.

Depression

Research suggests that one in five young people aged 16–24 years suffers from depression that is distressing enough to justify seeking professional help. The symptoms can range from an ongoing low mood and lack of energy to severe disruptions to sleep and appetite, extreme mood swings and suicidal thinking.

Any such condition impacts on a young person's ability to get through their day, and can erode the foundation of relationships with family, friends and teachers.

A 2018 study from the UK found that Year 7 girls seem to have a much higher rate of depression than boys. This seems closely linked to the amount of time they spend on social media, along with the impact of online bullying and poor sleep, which, in combination, contribute to this low mood. As many as three-quarters of Year 7 girls who suffer from depression were also found to have low self-esteem, were unhappy with how they looked, and slept for seven hours or less each night. The study was based on interviews with almost 11 000 14-year-olds who were taking part in the Millennium Cohort Study, a major research project into children's lives.

While clinical experience suggests that early diagnosis and timely treatment are effective, many young people who experience a mental disorder never seek professional help. This is because many young people do not know where to go for help, and parents and teachers don't know what signs to look for.

Depression warning signs

- Frequent, unexplained sadness or tearfulness
- Persistent low energy
- A preoccupation with morbid or lawless themes
- Lack of connection with family and friends
- Extreme sensitivity to rejection or failure
- Increased irritability, anger or hostility
- Frequent complaints of physical illnesses, such as stomach aches or, in the case of girls, menstrual problems
- Major changes in eating or sleeping habits
- Self-destructive or self-harming behaviours

What to do

- Try to engage your child in conversation, and listen carefully to what they say
- Encourage regular exercise and good sleep habits, and a healthy diet
- Seek help from a GP, and obtain a full physical examination with blood tests
- Encourage your child to take part in activities that once gave them pleasure (such as walks, movies), and be gently insistent if your invitation is refused

- Don't dismiss their behaviour as 'normal' adolescent mood swings
- Don't dismiss or ridicule the feelings they express, but point out realities and offer hope
- Don't accuse them of faking illness, or expect them to 'snap out of it'
- Don't ignore any remarks about suicide: report them to a GP or psychologist as soon as possible. If you feel the situation is urgent, ring 000 immediately.

In many cases, seeing a mental health professional (psychologist, counsellor or psychiatrist) is sufficient to help a young person recover from depression. In more severe cases, it may be necessary to consider medication, though this decision must always be made under the guidance of a psychiatrist or paediatrician.

Eating disorders

This generation is more media savvy than any preceding it and has been raised on images of sassy 'girl heroes'. At the same time, fashion's ideal stick-thin look can cause body image problems and eating disorders. There are several factors that affect eating behaviours during adolescence, including changing body shape and increased self-awareness, new sexual feelings and risk-taking tendencies. In addition, there is the ubiquitous media imagery that encourages unrealistic body image. While the proportion of the population that is overweight is increasing, young people are surrounded on all sides by images of 'ideal' but impossibly thin body shapes.

There are two types of eating disorders that are most likely to begin in adolescence, and below are some warning signs to look out for. Anorexia nervosa, which affects 0.5–1 per cent of young women, is a serious and potentially life-threatening illness involving the restriction of food intake and weight. Bulimia nervosa, which affects 1–5 per cent of young women, is characterised by repeated episodes of binge eating followed by compensatory behaviours, such as vomiting or excessive exercise. Most of the common known risk factors for eating disorders apply to both males and females (e.g. perfectionism, bullying, dieting, trauma, childhood obesity). Sociocultural influences play a role in the development of eating disorders, and cultural messages can increase vulnerability towards developing an eating disorder. This messaging can be that you should only have one body type, you need to be in control, and you are what you look like. Young people are more at risk if they conflate having a 'perfect body' with success in other areas such as dating, getting a good job, and social desirability.

Eating disorder warning signs

- A marked increase or decrease in weight with no medical cause
- The rise of abnormal eating habits, such as severe dieting or secretive bingeing
- An extreme preoccupation with weight and body image
- Compulsive or excessive exercising
- Self-induced vomiting, or excessive use of laxatives, diet pills or diuretics

Young people with an eating disorder are often 'in denial' and will most likely reject offers of help, preferring to isolate themselves. They may be on the constant lookout for opportunities to secretly exercise and to hide food rather than consume it, which can make it very difficult for parents looking for warning signs.

What to do

- Remain composed and always talk calmly
- Seek professional help
- Don't blame yourself or your parenting
- Don't blame your child for what is going on, and never give up on them, no matter how difficult things get
- Don't comment on your child's appearance. Whatever you say, it's likely to be misinterpreted.
- Don't try to force your child to eat, or make mealtimes a major drama. If you are working with a health professional, you will have a strategy for how supportive and assertive you need to be at meal times – and importantly, what your child knows they can expect from you.

Self-harm

The term 'self-harm' is most often associated with cutting but it can also involve overdosing on over-the-counter and prescription drugs, swallowing harmful chemicals such as bleach, or banging or hitting oneself. Self-harm is profoundly worrying to many Year 7 parents. Most parents whose child is self-harming are terrified that their child wants to end their life, but in the vast majority of cases it has nothing to do with suicidal ideation (although it may appear to). In most cases the young people are trying to distract themselves from overwhelming emotional pain. In my experience, many young people who self-harm are using it to try to cope with destructive relationships at home or school, or some kind of emotional trauma such as a break-up, the death of a relative or other pressures.

Among the Year 7s I work with, self-harming students commonly make small cuts on their body, usually the arms and legs, which helps them control their emotional pain. Cuts can be easily hidden under long sleeves, and this practice has existed for a long time in secrecy. But in recent years, social media and movies have drawn attention to it, prompting greater numbers of teens and tweens (ages 9 to 14) to try it.

Year 7s often keep self-harm to themselves because of shame or fear of discovery. If they are cutting themselves, they may cover up their skin and avoid discussing the problem. It's often up to close family and friends to notice when young people are self-harming, and to take them to a GP or mental health professional, or approach the subject with care and understanding.

Self-harm is not just 'attention seeking', although some students do use it as a way of letting others know they aren't coping. Other reasons young people have given for their self-harm include: trying to express complicated or hidden feelings, communicating a need for some support, proving to themselves that they are not invisible, feeling in control, and getting an immediate sense of relief.

Unsurprisingly, parents confronted with a child who is self-harming generally become very frightened, confused, angry and panicked. It is crucial that you do not share these reactions with your child. Chances are they are already feeling isolated, helpless and desperate, and they need you to be strong enough to assist them in getting help.

It is important not to ignore their self-harming, as there is a good chance they may be experiencing anxiety or depression. If they stop self-harming, they may replace this behaviour with an eating disorder, abusing cough medications, drinking or taking drugs/alcohol. Self-harm is never the whole picture. On a brighter note, many young people simply 'grow out' of self-harming, and go on to establish meaningful relationships: in a 2011 study by The Lancet of 1 800 subjects, researchers found that of the 136 who reported harming themselves as teens, 90 per cent reported no further self-harm as young adults.

Self-harm: warning signs

- Small straight lines, often parallel like railroad ties, carved into the forearm, upper arm or sometimes the legs
- Scratching or biting the skin
- Burning their skin with lit matches, cigarettes or other hot, sharp objects
- Hitting or punching themselves or the walls
- Piercing their skin with sharp objects
- Pulling out hair
- Picking at scabs and wounds
- Banging head or body against walls and hard objects

What to do

- Try to stay calm, be a role model and show that you can manage your difficult emotions.

- Act on your instincts. If you suspect that your child is self-harming, ask them: 'Have you ever felt so bad that you have hurt yourself on purpose?' Upon discovery, ask: 'What happened?' Reassure them that you understand and are going to get them professional help; tell them it's going to be okay.
- Offer a hug (for at least 20 seconds). If your hug request is denied, you can hug with your words – try whispering a polite, lovely 'thank you' with a smile. It will mean everything.
- Find an experienced mental health professional via a local Headspace centre or another child and adolescent mental health service to help.

Suicide and suicidal behaviours

Suicide is the leading cause of death for young Australians aged 15–24 years old, with hundreds of young people dying each year. Suicide and suicidal thinking are associated with a variety of biological, social and psychological factors, including traumatic life events and/or mental health conditions, such as depression, anxiety disorders, and borderline personality disorder. Resilience, self-esteem, connectedness, feelings of belonging, supportive environments and positive life events can be valuable safeguards against the effects of trauma and mental health conditions. Parents need to realise that most suicidal young people don't want to die. Rather, they are usually experiencing extreme distress and/or unbearable pain and can't think of another way to cope. With support, they can find ways to manage their distress and get through the crisis.

Completed suicide is a relatively rare event, particularly for young women. However, in 2011, the Australian Bureau of Statistics reported that the number of people taking their own lives had increased by 43 per cent since 2006. Although still lower than the levels of male suicide, the number of young women aged 15–19 years who completed suicide has almost doubled over this time.

While it is clear that young people in Australia are more knowledgeable about mental health issues than they were a generation ago, it seems that knowledge is not enough. An opportunity exists to build on this knowledge with concise instructions about seeking help, stress and wellness management, and crisis support. This must include strategies that embrace the use of new and emerging technologies. Instead of demonising smartphone apps, wearable devices and social media, we need to use this technology to reach those most at risk, including people who are unemployed, homeless, Indigenous, disabled, lesbian, gay, bisexual, transgender, intersex, queer, asexual (LGBTIQA) and those who are geographically isolated.

The good news is that many suicides in early adolescents can be prevented if warning signs are detected and appropriate intervention is conducted. While one size does not fit all, there are some common reasons why a Year 7 might consider suicide.The 2015 report on the second Australian Child and Adolescent Survey of Mental Health and Wellbeing found that the vast majority of young people (9 out of 10) who take their own life have an underlying mental illness, such as depression.

Some of the Year 7s with an existing mental health problem will attempt suicide if faced with an acute crisis, which might be a reaction to some conflict with peers or parents that is magnified in their mind. Such conflicts are common among teens, but those who attempt suicide are particularly reactive to them because they:

- Have a long-standing history of problems at home or school
- Have experienced a trauma
- Have been the victim of physical, sexual or emotional abuse
- Suffer from low self-esteem
- Believe no one cares
- Are depressed
- Abuse alcohol or drugs

Suicide: Warning signs

- Noticeable changes in eating or sleeping habits
- Unexplained, or unusually severe, violent or rebellious behaviour
- Withdrawal from family or friends
- Sexual promiscuity, truancy, and vandalism
- Drastic personality change
- Agitation, restlessness, distress, or panicky behaviour
- Talking or writing about committing suicide, even jokingly
- Giving away prized possessions
- Doing worse in school

What to do

If you notice any of these warning signs in your Year 7, you should take these steps:

- Have a courageous conversation: Tell them what you have noticed, express your concern and ask your Year 7 directly whether they are thinking of killing themselves.

If they say yes, ask how long they have been thinking about this, whether they have a plan and whether they have a time frame in mind. Seek professional help immediately. Talking about suicide doesn't cause suicide – but avoiding what's on their mind may increase their feelings of isolation and hopelessness.

- Offer help and listen: don't ignore the problem. What you've noticed may be your child's way of crying out for help. Having a caring and non-judgemental attitude can encourage the start of a meaningful conversation.

- Remove any means of taking their own lives in your home. Secure pills, kitchen utensils, ropes or poisons which might be used as a means to commit suicide.

- Get professional help from a GP or your local Headspace centre. A Year 7 at risk of suicide needs professional help. Even when the immediate crisis passes, the risk of suicidal behaviour remains high until new ways of dealing and coping with problems are learned.

- Don't be afraid to take your Year 7 to a hospital accident and emergency department. If it is clear that they are planning suicide you may not be able to handle the situation on your own.

When your child expresses concern about a friend who is struggling with mental illness

Part of being in a secondary school community means that your Year 7 will most likely have a wide circle of friends over the course of their schooling. It is likely, at some stage, that they will have a

friend who may be experiencing anxiety, self-harming or express-
ing suicidal tendencies. This can place undue stress on your child
and it is not their burden to carry. If your adolescent comes to you
with concerns about a friend's mental health, firstly, thank them
for having the courage to tell you. Reassure them that they have
done the right thing by coming to you. Issues of mental health
can be serious and need the assistance of a trained professional. If
this student is at your child's school, make contact with the year
level coordinator via email or a phone call and relay your child's
concern. Explain gently to your child that this is not a burden to
carry alone. The best way they can help their friend is by telling a
trusted adult who can ensure that help can be provided.

Many students reveal that they are afraid to tell an adult, as they
feel they will risk losing the friendship, or that their friend will hate
them for telling someone. It is important that young people get the
message that the way their friend will get better is by having adults
working with them to get through the issue. Their friend will
hopefully one day thank them for caring so much.

The key message for all Year 7 parents reading this book is
that the vast majority of young people who take their own lives
have a history of mental illness – some diagnosed, some not. The
most common mental illness associated with suicide is depression.
So, suicide prevention is really all about depression awareness.
Early diagnosis and prompt treatment of suicidal behaviours and
depression combined with good follow-up is essential. But an even
better way to deal with this is to help your child build, from a
young age, the skills, knowledge and strategies they will need to
cope with life.

KEEPING YOUR CHILD SAFE

Getting to know other parents

In primary school you are very likely to get to know fellow parents in your child's social group through playdates, birthday parties and the occasional parent evening. Conversely, secondary school can feel more isolating as a parent. While some secondary schools try to counteract this by offering welcome morning teas and parent information evenings for new parents, it can take some effort to establish new relationships with parents of your secondary schooler's friends.

Just as is the case in primary school, developing some form of communication or relationship with other secondary school parents can be beneficial for a number of reasons, including:

- the opportunity to get to know the family situations of your secondary schooler's friends, and whether they have similar values to you
- the opportunity for carpooling situations should the need arise
- developing your own group for support as your children journey through secondary school together and begin their adolescent years
- general support in the case of emergencies, illness in the family etc.

DAYLIGHT SAVINGS, DAD. WE **GAIN AN HOUR!**

Your Year 7's social life

A book written for parents about helping their child navigate their foray into secondary school wouldn't be complete without a discussion of the social activities, parties and gatherings they will inevitably be invited to. It may not happen in Year 7, but it is highly likely, depending on their social circle.

Case study

When Lara was in secondary school, all the members of her class were invited to attend a fifteenth birthday party, which involved a forty-minute train trip to the girl's home. Every guest travelled on the train except for Lara, because her parents insisted that she be driven to and from the birthday party. Suffice to say Lara was fairly cheesed off about being the odd one out. The party ended up being a perfectly safe one, however, Lara's parents reserved their right to set the rules and enforce them, particularly as it was one of the first 'large' parties she had been invited to. While Lara was annoyed, she did not suffer because of this boundary and she was invited to plenty more parties.

This is where you come in as their parent or caregiver. It is your job to know what your secondary schooler's social plans are and to be involved in them. It is imperative that you lay the ground rules and guidelines for attending social events: transport to and from the event, curfews, expected behaviour, and restricted items such as drugs and alcohol. You might be surprised that I have included a reference to alcohol and drug use in a book to help your Year 7 find their feet in secondary school. Although the 2016 National Drug Strategy Household Survey found that 77.8 per cent of 12–17-year-olds have never had a full serve of alcohol, it also found that 1.4 per cent drink weekly (while for the 18–24 age group, the figure is 28.7 per cent).

At the risk of causing unnecessary alarm, you simply must be aware that there are young people who do have access to drugs and alcohol, even as young as Year 7. And while you may be paying in excess of $30 000 per year to send your secondary schooler to a prestigious school, this does not guarantee that every student will be of a reputable nature. Thus, it is imperative that you put some non-negotiables in place before your child extends their social schedule. These should include:

Meet the parents

Yes, your secondary schooler may threaten to disown you and tell you that *no one else's parent* would do something that embarrassing, but this is part of your parenting duty. You take your child to the party location, meet the parents and pick up your child at the designated time (unless you have made other suitable arrangements with a parent you know).

Parents must be in attendance at the party/gathering

How do you find out if parents will be there? You call them. You ask your child for the parents' contact details. (A 17-year-old sibling won't cut it.) This is not weird, this is responsible parenting.

Curfew

Negotiate this with your offspring, however, remember they are still young. They need their sleep. Arrange a suitable time that you will collect your child and stick to this.

X plan

A few years ago I came across an excellent idea that gives young people a 'get out of jail free' card, if you like. It is used for a young person who finds themselves in an awkward or potentially dangerous situation when they need a parent or caregiver to provide a way out and collect them.

It is a predetermined plan that if your child sends a text message with just the letter 'X', the parent or caregiver immediately knows that their child needs to be picked up. The agreement stipulates that there will be no angry outbursts or immediate retribution (discipline can come later if needed). Your child knows that they can count on you to come and pick them up without fear of looking silly or 'lame' in front of their peers.

It goes like this:

Jack finds himself at a party where there are no parents present and copious amounts of alcohol are being consumed. He feels unsafe and is being pressured into drinking. He sends a text to his mum that simply reads, 'X'.

Mum reads this text and makes a call to Jack within the next five minutes. Jack answers and hears his mum say that she has received his text and for Jack to send through the address of the party. Jack, on picking up the call from his mum, speaks out loud (in front of his peers if needed) something like this:

'Hi, Mum. What's up? What? What's happened? Why do I have to be picked up though? That's not fair! Can you tell me now? Oh, okay. See you soon.'

Then he says to his mates:

'Sorry, guys. I have to go. Something's happened, and I have to be picked up.'

It's a great plan and one that takes the stress off all concerned. You should set this plan up with your secondary schooler as soon as possible, and involve other close carers such as grandparents as well. It doesn't matter who receives the 'X' as long as they know how to respond. As a parent myself, I would much rather receive a text from one of my children that they are in a precarious situation and need to be picked up, no questions asked, than receive a knock on the door from a police officer in the early hours of the morning.

What the students have to say . . .

I wish that my parents knew that just because I don't share things or tell them what I'm feeling doesn't mean that I don't trust them or that it's their fault. Sometimes I'm not ready to tell my parents things or I may think it's something I can handle on my own and I don't want them to get close and know all my business because that's stressful. Sometimes, it's better for them to wait until I feel comfortable to tell them. (Unless they can really tell that things are really bad.)

Frank

I wish my parents knew how stressful everything was, even though I was in a support program. And I wish they knew how much my not-so-great friends were affecting my mental health. Going to a counsellor helped, but I wasn't really talking to my parents.

Kate

TAKEAWAYS FROM THIS SECTION

There are options if your child is experiencing problems at secondary school.

- Keep the lines of communication open
  Communicate with the school, particularly if you are finding that secondary school is hard going for your child. If they are struggling, know that there are always alternatives to be looked at and plans that can be put in place to ease the pressure on your child if needed.

- Changing schools
  Sometimes you may find that the secondary school your child began at isn't the best fit for them, for a whole host of reasons. Know that this is not a complete disaster. Many children have moved schools during secondary school and this has been a game changer for them.

- Monitor your child's mental health
  If you notice extreme changes in your child's mood, sleeping or eating habits, it may well be worth a visit to your GP. Always investigate what is going on for your child and seek urgent help when needed. There is a great deal of support out there to help you and your child. You are never alone.

A final word

Thanks for taking the time to read this book.

Our main takeaways are:

- Planning is key.
- Try to help your Year 7 to keep doing the things they like to do.
- Remind them that it probably won't be amazing straight away – they may need to lower their expectations.
- Talking to new people is hard, but it is worth it – the greatest predictor of wellbeing in Year 7 is a rich repertoire of friends.
- Your child can and should reach out if it gets too much.

Our hope for your Year 7 is that they won't just survive secondary school, but that they will thrive! Secondary school can be what they decide to make of it: it can be a fantastic and amazing stage of their life if they just embrace all the changes that it brings. And even though they might go through some bumpy patches, challenges and growth, remember this: secondary school won't last forever, and hopefully they will come through the end of it with some great memories. Above all we want to remind you that there is no such thing as a perfect parent. Both of us made mistakes when we were bringing up our children but we truly hope that this book will help you to make fewer yourself as your child enters Year 7. It is important to remember that three-quarters of young people going into Year 7 not only survive the transition but thrive. Following the tips in our book will greatly increase the odds of your child being part of that majority.

Resources

Reach Out
www.reachout.com.au

Beyond Blue
www.beyondblue.com.au

CyberSafety Solutions
www.cybersafetysolutions.com.au

Kids Helpline
www.kidshelpline.com.au

Raising Children
www.raisingchildren.net.au

Moodgym
www.moodgym.com.au

Helpful resources to help your ASD child navigate secondary school:

Book: *The Advocacy Project* by Spectrum Journeys

www.spectrumjourneys.org.au

The I Can Network

www.icannetwork.com.au

Yellow Lady Bugs

www.yellowladybugs.com.au

Occupational Therapy

www.theottoolbox.com

Acknowledgements

Michael Carr-Gregg

Starting Secondary School could not have happened without the support of my co-author, friend and legendary teacher, Sharon Witt. I am indebted to her for her support, wisdom and experience, which she has shared so beautifully in this book. I'd also like to thank Ali Watts for her unfailing support in helping me publish this eleventh book for Penguin Random House, and for sticking by the Hawthorn Football Club. Sharon and I are both grateful to Fay Helfenbaum for some superb literary panel-beating and for having the patience of a saint while we responded to her editing requests. Finally I'd like to acknowledge all those students who are about to embark on the great adventure that is secondary school. Remember: see life as it is and focus on the good bits.

Sharon Witt

What an honour it has been to work on such an exciting project with Dr Michael Carr-Gregg, my friend, mentor and someone I have always held in such high regard. I can't think of anyone more qualified to co-author a book about guiding adolescents through secondary school, and I hope this book is the first of many. This has been such a positive experience for both of us, and I cannot give enough thanks to the amazing Ali Watts from Penguin Random House for her guidance and encouragement throughout the entire process. Many thanks to Fay Helfenbaum and Amanda Martin for their editing prowess and for helping make this book the best it can be.

To the wonderful students I have had the pleasure of teaching in secondary school over the past twenty-eight years: you have all left an imprint on my heart.

To my own gorgeous young people, Josh and Emily, thank you for always cheering me on. And to my greatest cheerleader, Andy – you are forever missed.

Index